# IN PURSUIT OF THE PIC

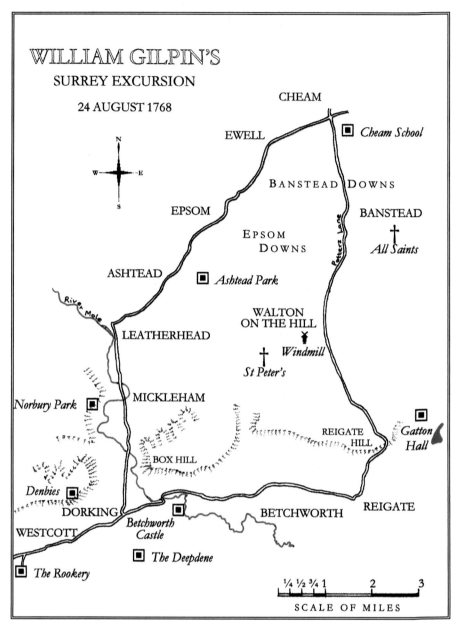

# WILLIAM GILPIN'S

## SURREY EXCURSION

### 24 AUGUST 1768

N

W—E

S

CHEAM

EWELL

Cheam School

BANSTEAD DOWNS

BANSTEAD

EPSOM

EPSOM DOWNS

All Saints

Peters Lane

ASHTEAD

Ashtead Park

River Mole

WALTON ON THE HILL

LEATHERHEAD

Windmill

St Peter's

Norbury Park

MICKLEHAM

REIGATE HILL

Gatton Hall

BOX HILL

Denbies

DORKING

Betchworth Castle

BETCHWORTH

REIGATE

WESTCOTT

The Deepdene

The Rookery

¼ ½ ¾ 1    2    3

SCALE OF MILES

SKETCH MAP SHOWING THE ROUTE OF WILLIAM GILPIN'S EXCURSION IN SURREY,
ALONG POTTER'S LANE, VIA REIGATE AND DORKING TO THE ROOKERY,
AND HIS RETURN TO CHEAM THROUGH MICKLEHAM AND ASHTEAD

# IN PURSUIT OF THE PICTURESQUE

## WILLIAM GILPIN'S
## SURREY EXCURSION

### THE PLACES HE PASSED
### AND THEIR CLAIMS TO FAME

JOAN PERCY

SURREY GARDENS TRUST

First published in Great Britain in 2001 by
SURREY GARDENS TRUST

DESIGN by MARION WOODWARD

ILLUSTRATIONS RESEARCH by BRENDA LEWIS

British Library Cataloguing in Publication Data.
A catalogue record for this book is available
from the British Library

ISBN 0 9540630 0 7

Printed and bound by Unwin Brothers Limited,
The Gresham Press, Old Woking, Surrey GU22 9LH

# CONTENTS

# ACKNOWLEDGEMENTS

Our considerable debt to many people and institutions will be evident in the text and notes, but particular thanks must go to Dr. Christopher Wright of the British Library for his most helpful advice, to Julian Pooley and the Surrey History Centre for the wealth of material put at our disposal, to the British Museum, to Pam Porter of the British Library for assistance with the Stopes' papers, and to Dr. Stopes-Roe; to Peter Nutley and Janet Wood for their drawings, to David Webb for our journey round the Rookery grounds, to Joan Collins and Patience Gapper of the Surrey Gardens Trust, and to Elizabeth Dixon, Eileen England and Roger Young.

We are also grateful to Surrey County Council and Mole Valley District Council for their generous grants towards the cost of publication.

## SURREY GARDENS TRUST

The Surrey Gardens Trust is a registered educational charity, founded in 1991, to help identify, preserve and recreate the county's outstanding gardens and landscapes, large and small, and to increase awareness of this heritage. It is part of a countrywide network of Trusts and is financed by subscriptions, grants and donations.

For further information about the Trust, visit our website at:

www.surreyweb.org.uk/surrey-gardens-trust

# FOREWORD

Mavis Batey, President of the Garden History Society until July 2000, first drew the attention of the Surrey Gardens Trust to William Gilpin's manuscript of his 1768 tour and she has generously contributed this Foreword on William Gilpin and the evolution of the Picturesque.

THE Picturesque is a peculiarly English phenomenon, a mode of vision set in train by an obscure parson/schoolmaster, the Revd. William Gilpin, who taught at Cheam in Surrey; its legacy is still felt in landscape architecture and town and country planning. Gilpin did not set out to formulate an abstract theory of the Picturesque, however; that would be developed later by the two Herefordshire squires Uvedale Price and Richard Payne Knight. His was essentially a practical mission to teach the study of pictures and to offer the 'amusement' of picturesque travel. Jane Austen, who was 'enamoured of the Picturesque' describes the result perfectly when she reports that the fashionable Tilneys were 'viewing the country with the eyes of people accustomed to painting and deciding on its capabilities of being made into pictures'. By then all persons of taste were eager to draw, collect prints and take part in the picturesque discovery of Britain. Gilpin, who had started the craze, being thoroughly versed in the principles of painting, had set out in the school holidays 'in search of the Picturesque' and made observations and on-the-spot sketches.

Alexander Pope was the first to use the expression picturesque in English when he spoke of the 'imaging and picturesque parts of Homer' and the word was clearly synonymous with scenes 'painted to the mind' when reading epic or pastoral poetry. Gilpin was much influenced by Pope and he encouraged his pupils to cultivate a 'picture-making faculty' when reading descriptive passages in the classics. He listed for them what he found picturesque in Virgil's *Aeneid* - a hero resting after battle, a sea nymph pushing a ship, a wolf running away in fear; these were heroic attitudes suitable for history painting, not necessarily connected with landscape, but consistent with Pope's use of the word picturesque as verbal painting. At the same time, in the 1750s, Gilpin was working on his *Essay on Prints*, the first standard guide for the instruction of the new large public for whom cheap prints had become available. In his Essay he defines picturesque, once and for all, as 'that kind of beauty which is agreeable in a picture'.

From cultivating a picture imagination when reading and studying and evaluating prints it had been an easy step for Gilpin to suggest that the traveller should use the same faculty in viewing real landscape. As a Cumbrian, Gilpin's predilection was for lakes and mountains and he delighted in out-of-the-way rugged scenes in the Wye Valley, Snowdonia, the Peaks, the Lakes and the Highlands. Although these journeys were made from Cheam in the holidays in the 1770s, it was not until after he had left the school and moved to the New Forest that he was persuaded by his friends to publish his picturesque tours, which were immediately popular. His *Lakes Tour*, published in 1786, was sold out in a few days. Roads had greatly improved and picturesque travel soon became a favourite pastime, and with so much unrest on the continent even the nobility were forced to make the home tour.

Gilpin's 'Rygate - Dorking' tour, now in print for the first time, is of great interest as it was written in 1768, the year Gilpin's *Essay on Prints* was published. His ideas of applying the principles of analysing the constituent parts of a landscape in a print to picturesque observations in travel were just beginning to take shape. He wanted the tourist to break down the scenes that pleased him into such picturesque components as stillness, roughness, inequality of surfaces, strong lights and shades, the gleam of water or tints on hills and to look for a foreground feature which would enhance or frame the picture; the picturesque spot chosen for sketching or capturing in a landscape mirror or just observing was called a 'station'. The Dorking notebook notes 'beautiful objects' such as church spires and windmills, particularly praising Betchworth castle, 'rising among wood . . . [which] puts you in mind of Poussin'. Foregrounds, distances, middle distances, sidescreens are all noted from the chosen station. On the way from Reigate, Gilpin points out one such spot, where there is 'a good foreground of trees, and broken ground, with a winding road, a first distance of woody hedgerows well grouped and shapen; beyond them a second distance of rising ground'.

William Gilpin never intended his picturesque principles to be applied to landscape gardening as Uvedale Price was later to do in his *Essay on the Picturesque* in 1794 which bore the sub-title 'on the use of Studying Pictures for the Purpose of Improving Real Landscape'. Gilpin did have a considerable influence on the high phase of landscape gardening, however. Loudon's *Encyclopaedia* of 1820 recommended that 'the whole of his tours and writings on the Picturesque will merit the study of the landscape gardener'. Gilpin had given his readers the concept of regional characteristics ('how variously Nature works up landscape') which caused a reaction to systematized landscape gardening where a formula could be applied in any county without regard to the character of the area.

One specific Gilpin-inspired landscape gardening feature was the circuit walk, which his friend and ally, the Revd. William Mason, based on his picturesque tour ideas. It was chiefly Mason who persuaded Gilpin to publish his tours, the first of which on the Wye in 1782 was dedicated to him. The two picturesque parsons kept up a regular correspondence and always showed each other the draft of their writings before publication. Mason had hoped that his friend would write a prose version of his long poem *The English Garden*, in which he sets out instructions for picturesque circuit walks but this he declined to do. The early landscape gardens such as Stowe, Studley Royal, or Stourhead, had walks with designed vistas but these were orientated on man-made scenery and buildings, especially temples, whereas picturesque circuit walks looked beyond the garden into natural scenery with the prospect broken down into a series of framed peephole scenes; these viewpoints corresponded to the stations Gilpin recommended to picturesque tourists. The best examples of this feature were to be seen in the grounds of three of Gilpin's patrons, Lord Harcourt of Nuneham Courtenay in Oxfordshire, William Mitford of Exbury in Hampshire and William Lock of Norbury in Surrey. Jane Austen gives Mr Darcy such a picturesque circuit walk at Pemberley in Derbyshire to show the prejudiced heroine that he is a man of taste.

Interestingly enough, we have an example of before and after treatment of a landscaped garden at Norbury, described by Gilpin, although he was too modest to suggest that it had been influenced by his ideas. When he describes Norbury in the 1768 MS Notebook before the property was acquired by Lock his only comment is that there is 'a rising lawn of firm turf ornamented with clumps', which was typical of a mid-century Capability Brown style park. When Gilpin visited again in 1775 he saw his friend's new picturesque layout with its fine circuit walk in the making and, in his revised *Western Tour*, not published until 1798, when the landscaped garden had matured, he describes some of the stations and peephole scenes. 'Through the woods, a walk is conducted along its sloping side; from whence you have descending views into the vale below, some of which seen through the spreading arms of an oak or a beech, as through the frame of a picture, have a pleasing effect. The other side of the side-screen of the vale consists of that boast of Surrey, the celebrated Box Hill'.

It is good to know that Surrey County Council is restoring the Norbury woodland walk which delighted Gilpin and the publication of this book can only add to the enjoyment of the Dorking area for today's residents and picturesque tourist.

*Mavis Batey*
*Past President of The Garden History Society*

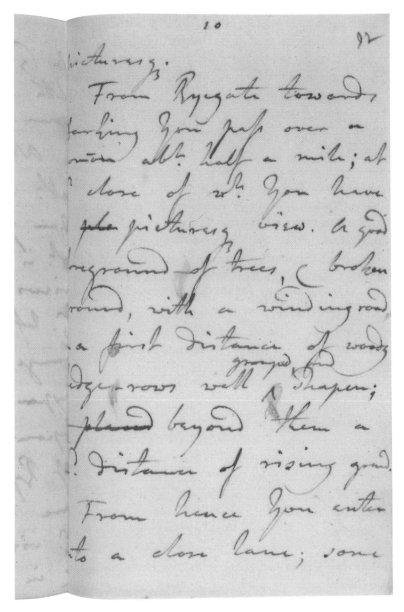

# THE MANUSCRIPT

G ILPIN'S comments on his journey from Cheam to the Rookery and back are written in one of his memorandum books, and form part of MS. Eng. misc. e. 522 held at the Bodleian Library, which includes his notes on his visit to Kew and his first visit to Painshill, together with some other jottings. Measuring about 19 x 11 centimetres (7.5 x 4.4 inches), the right-hand pages are used for the main text and the left hand for later additions or corrections.

## THE TEXT

The complete text, as William Gilpin wrote it, is followed, but is first divided into sections which precede the chapters, so that the commentaries can be more readily connected with his descriptions. It is repeated, without any division, in the Appendix for those interested in reading the account straight through. Gilpin's spelling is kept except for abbreviations such as 'shd', or 'comon' (common); 'y^e', the written version usual in his time for 'the', is given its modern form.

It has to be remembered that Gilpin's manuscript, even with its corrections and additions, is only his first text. He took pride in his writing and would have altered such things as repetitive phrasing, for example, when making a final version. He was very upset later when Mrs Delany lent out a copy of one of his *Tours* which he had not had time to revise properly.

## ACKNOWLEDGEMENT

The Surrey Gardens Trust is most grateful to the Bodleian Library, University of Oxford, for permission to transcribe William Gilpin's manuscript.

PORTRAIT OF WILLIAM GILPIN IN 1781 BY H. WALTON

# CHAPTER I - INTRODUCTION
## WILLIAM GILPIN, HIS LIFE AND BACKGROUND

WHEN William Gilpin rode over the Downs past Reigate and Dorking to Westcott and then back to Cheam in 1768, he was embarking on one of his first summer holiday excursions which led to his amazingly successful publications - his series of 'picturesque' tours. The record of his expedition with its accompanying drawings is relatively brief, yet it shares much of the thinking of those later accounts. Moreover, the landscape he appraises and the places he mentions can be compared with their later history, so that no-one interested in the Surrey area that was his home ground for over two decades can fail to enjoy his observations.

Gilpin was no native of Surrey however; his love of the countryside was nurtured in Cumberland. Born in 1724, he grew up at Scaleby Castle, north of Carlisle, where his parents lived with his grandfather, William Gilpin, as his father, John Bernard Gilpin, was in the army and often away. After grandfather William's death, John Bernard moved his family to Carlisle itself and neither he nor his elder son, William, ever lost their love of the varied and rugged country around. 'If you had seen as many lakes and mountains as I have seen, they would put everything else out of your head',

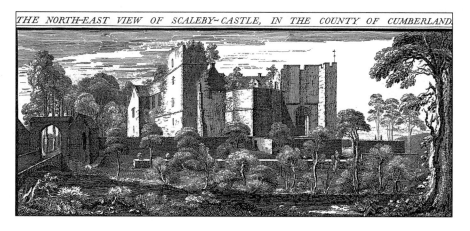

SCALEBY CASTLE, ENGRAVING BY S. AND N. BUCK (1739)
SCALEBY WAS PURCHASED BY WILLIAM GILPIN'S GREAT GRAND-FATHER WHO BEAUTIFIED
THE PART-RUINOUS CASTLE WITH HIS PLANTING. NEGLECTED AT VARIOUS TIMES SINCE,
IT WAS LAST RESTORED IN 1952 BY THE FATHER OF THE PRESENT OWNER, LORD HENLEY

wrote William late in life to a friend, Mary Hartley.[1] For him they were 'rich volumes' bearing 'constant perusal'.[2] Comparable to this attachment was his deep interest in art, passed on by his father to both his sons. John Bernard, a considerable and life-long amateur artist himself, had taught William to draw from an early age and encouraged his appreciation of paintings and of what were more accessible, prints, which Gilpin started to buy, he records, 'as a mere boy'.[3] His first purchase was a landscape by Waterloo[4] and an etching by Rembrandt, and he continued to add to them while at university (Queen's College, Oxford) and afterwards in London, so that by his late twenties he had a considerable collection, but not however an expensive one, as his means were small. He learnt the technique of etching in the 1740s and he continued to draw, writing to his mother in 1742 that, whenever he went walking, he always took his paper and black-

DICTIS FACTISQVE SIMPLEX

GILPIN FAMILY CREST

lead pencil and 'never failed to bring home something or other'.[5] His brother, Sawrey (1733-1807), became a professional painter, well-known for his horse-painting and was elected a Royal Academician in 1797.

William chose to enter the Church, a decision springing from his deep faith, not expediency. He was ordained deacon in 1746, completed his degree in 1748 and held two if not three curacies before 1752. When we read of him then or during his years in Cheam or, finally, in Hampshire, we gain the impression of a devout Christian careful for all both in daily life and by means of his religious and other serious writings. His biographies of Bernard Gilpin, the 'Apostle of the North' (1752)[6] and of other Reformers such as Hugh Latimer, were appreciatively reviewed and popular. But Gilpin is remembered today for his enduring leisure interest which remained, as in his youth, in Nature and in Art, with all the details of the relationship between them.

For his first publication on this topic we go back to 1748 when there appeared anonymously[7] *A Dialogue upon the Gardens of the Right Honourable the Lord Viscount Cobham, at Stow in Buckinghamshire.* Gilpin had been preaching at Buckingham and had easy opportunity to see the already famous and beautiful grounds of Stowe. In the preface to his pamphlet, Gilpin states 'the following Observations are not designed as a Description of the Place at all satisfactory to those who have not seen it, but to renew the Idea of it to those that have'. Thus he is unexpectedly, even if hindered a little by the style of his age, speaking to the many people today who have visited Stowe in the wake of the notable restoration work of the National Trust. We, too, can consider the Temple of Ancient Virtue and the 'poor shattered remains' of Modern Virtue and recall the 'variety of different shades among the trees, the lake spread so elegantly amongst them'. The two friends, the lover of beauty Callophilus and Polypthon the caviller, who conduct the dialogue on their walk, discuss the pictorial qualities of the 'landskip', the ways in which the edifices give point to the nearer views or the distant prospects and Polypthon, the more critical, cannot forbear a reference to Gilpin's favourite area. Had Lord Cobham had such materials to work with as he himself had recently enjoyed viewing in the north, he pointed out, 'it could not but be that he would make a most noble picture'.[8]

THE TEMPLE OF ANCIENT VIRTUE

'Making a noble picture' was very much in Gilpin's mind and in his 'Explanation of Terms' in his next work, the *Essay on Prints*, completed by 1753, he provides the term to encompass it - the picturesque - 'that kind of beauty which is agreeable in a picture'. This concept he adapted and refined as a result of his travels for many years after. Following his lead, the habit of picture-making when viewing landscape - seeking the picturesque - spread among tourists and lovers of the countryside everywhere. Meanwhile, his *Essay on Prints*, not published until 1768 and the earliest reference book of its kind, was widely acclaimed, quickly republished and by 1802 had gone into five editions and become well known abroad. It gave advice on collecting and appreciating prints as well as listing the main practitioners, stressing the need for the artists' constant referral to the 'characteristics of Nature'.

3

Regular opportunities for travelling round Great Britain came quite unexpectedly. In the early 1750s Gilpin met the Sanxays,[9] a Surrey family, in London. James Sanxay who was the Master of a school in Cheam was looking for a successor and asked Gilpin to take his place, which Gilpin eventually agreed to do. The school, of long standing, had been much respected. Gilpin recounts how it had removed from London to the purer air of Cheam at the time of the Great Plague. There it had flourished and by 1719, a house 'large and fit for the purpose' had been built[10] but it was now at a low ebb, James having married a wife without interest in the boarding and other domestic responsibilities. Numbers had dropped severely. Gilpin was more prudent in his choice of wife in his cousin Margaret, who supported him then and throughout a happy marriage.

Before he was able to make full use of his summer breaks, he had to re-build the fortunes of his school. So successful was he over the years that from fifteen pupils the number steadily climbed to nearly eighty with a waiting list, so that he was able in 1777, when he moved to Hampshire, to hand over a thriving establishment to his son William. His method of running the school was unusual for the time - corporal punishment was rare, Gilpin relying on a code of laws made clear to all boys, with any transgressions punished by a scale of detentions or fines. The fines were levied from the boys' weekly allowances, and projects for spending the accumulated money were discussed generally and spent on such things as extra seats for the playground, cricket bats and balls, or books for the

CHEAM SCHOOL. THE REAR ELEVATION IN 1834

4

library. Part of the money was set aside for bread for the poor which the boys distributed as being bought with their money. If any punishments or regulations appeared too harsh, a jury of twelve boys examined and pronounced on the case. By this means he impressed 'young minds with an early love of order, law and liberty'.

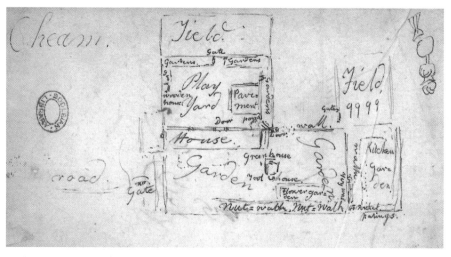

CHEAM SCHOOL - A ROUGH SKETCH, APPARENTLY BY A BOY, IN THE LATTER HALF OF THE EIGHTEENTH CENTURY. THE BOYS' GARDENS ARE TO THE SIDE OF THE PLAY YARD

He freed the curriculum from undue emphasis on the grammatical minutiae of the classical languages, giving more attention to our own tongue. Outside lessons he encouraged the cultivation of garden-plots which were much sought after and worked on, the boys producing melons, cucumbers and early salads, for example, and they constructed 'pleasant arbours' to sit in. He allowed some of the boys to keep little shops to sell gingerbread and apples and such like; if anything was neglected the privilege was withdrawn. A 'Promise Book' ensured that the boys could be entrusted outside the school and they rarely abused their trust.

Instruction in the Christian faith was of course important as was the study of the *New Testament*. William Gilpin's aim was to form the 'manners' of his pupils, based on a considered morality. He was highly critical of the licence of public schools where it was common for 'violence and oppression to be practised among schoolboys'. Some of the boys stayed on at Cheam throughout their whole career; others were sent on to public schools to finish their classical education. One such was Henry Addington, later Lord Sidmouth, who was sent to Winchester under Dr Warton.[11] He 'was so shocked at the wickedness he found [there]' that he ran away[12] and

5

was placed under a private tutor. It is interesting that a well-known modern biographical dictionary such as *Chambers* should say only that he was educated at Winchester College.

Not until the 1760s is there evidence through his drawings and his various notes to show that Gilpin was by then out and about with pen and pencil, recording different aspects of the landscape - on his way north to his family, for example; on a visit to Kent; to Norfolk, principally to see the paintings at Houghton collected by Sir Robert Walpole and also locally - as on his trip to Reigate and Dorking. His first *Tour* to be published, though not until 1782, was that made in 1770 when he travelled along the River Wye and into South Wales. This was followed by four other summer tours, one of which was to his favourite Cumberland and Westmorland. On his way he sketched and jotted down his 'Observations relative chiefly to picturesque beauty' in 'well-filled memorandum books', which he revised at leisure, entirely, as he stresses, for his own amusement and that of a few friends and indeed of their various connections.

Among these mainly well-known contemporaries was William Mason, the poet and writer, who thought highly of Gilpin's 'practised pencil' and 'eloquent pen' and said so to effect in his *Life* of his late friend Thomas Gray, of *Elegy Written in a Country Churchyard* fame. Shortly before his death in 1771, Gray had toured both the Wye Valley and the Lakes and had read with admiration Gilpin's account of the Wye and also felt how much the Journal he himself had kept in the Lake District needed illustrations. Echoing this, Mason wrote that the Revd. Mr Gilpin's work was completely satisfying 'because it is throughout assisted by masterly delineation', - no verbal skill on its own could match it. This commendation aroused much interest and Gilpin's transcripts were eagerly sought out and enjoyed, Horace Walpole, Mrs Delany and the Dowager Duchess of Portland being among the many appreciative readers; the account of his Lakes tour even reached George III and Queen Charlotte.[13] A doubtful Gilpin was eventually persuaded to risk publication of his *Tours*, choosing on Mason's advice to try out the *Wye Tour* as it had fewer expensive plates. These were engraved from his drawings by his nephew William Sawrey Gilpin[14] in aquatint. The publication later in 1782 was a great success and paved the way for his further ventures.

By this time William Gilpin was settled as a Vicar in Hampshire and preparing the manuscripts of his journeys for the press was carried out in circumstances very different from those at Cheam. On taking up the living of Boldre in the New Forest, he faced a scattered, neglected, even wild, parish which had no proper provision for the poor or instruction for the children. With characteristic care and zeal, he gradually re-built a sense of community in the area. He established a Sunday School for the children, at first in his own kitchen, and devised one of the earliest Friendly Societies with its insurance scheme for local women in need. And it was then that his *Tours* played a central part in Gilpin's plans for his parish. From their publication he was gaining significant profit and this he considered extraneous to his family's needs. With it he was able to realise his long-held dream of establishing a proper school-house. In 1791 the new building was completed with separate accommodation and curriculum for boys and girls and provision for two teachers. By 1793, he had gained support and part-funding for a new poor-house to replace the deplorable insanitary old building, secured its efficient running and ensured the self-respect of the occupants. Both initiatives became known nationally. All his activities were, as one would expect, in the framework of his Christian teaching.

BOLDRE CHURCH IN ITS RURAL SETTING (1838), ENGRAVED BY L. HAGHE
FROM A PAINTING BY J.M. GILBERT. GILPIN WOULD HAVE BEEN PLEASED WITH
THE PICTURESQUE GROUP OF THREE COWS IN THE RIGHT-HAND FOREGROUND

In one further way did he make his artistic talent serve his parish purposes. Realising from his friends' opinions that his drawings would command a sale, Gilpin began to assemble a large number and to sketch further picturesque landscapes. In 1802 these provided, together with other manuscripts, well in excess of £1,000. To his delight he was able to endow the local school fully, leaving enough money for current expenses.

Gilpin's new writing during his years at Boldre was, with one notable exception, no longer concerned with the Picturesque. This was his *Remarks on Forest Scenery* (1791) inspired by his growing love of the New Forest . He also put together his *Three Essays*, adding his poem on landscape painting (1794), the whole dedicated to his friend William Lock of Norbury Park. Otherwise his subjects were concerned with his parish and his moral teaching. He died on 4 April 1804, aged eighty, 'with great calmness and serenity'. Although his physical health had been impaired for some time, he was mentally very active and had continued with an extensive correspondence and to receive friends until the end.[15]

While his ethical writings had by their nature a limited life, his works on the Picturesque continued to be reprinted, added to posthumously and circulated abroad. His reputation as an initiator of picturesque travel grew, though to begin with not all his many followers realised that it was not topographical exactness that they would find in his illustrations. What he valued were compositional qualities; the balance of foreground, middle distance and background; contrast and variety; the ruggedness of the scene rather than any smooth elegance - and he did not hesitate to make and recommend to those sketching, appropriate adjustments. In detail the Picturesque meant the ivy-clad ruin rather than the symmetrical, finished edifice, the cowherd resting on his pole giving variety to the nearer view and not, with a moral message, the industrious labourer in a neatly cultivated field. Where animals were used, cows, he felt, should be chosen because of their colouring and shape, rather than the 'sleek horse'. A group of three cows was more picturesque as being less cumbersome than four. Interesting aquatints of these animals were included in the second part of

GILPIN'S SCHOOL, BOLDRE (1804), FROM A SKETCH BY GILPIN.
'UNITED TO IT [IS] A COMMODIOUS LITTLE MANSION FOR A MASTER. THE SCHOOL IS A HANDSOME ROOM, 25 FEET IN LENGTH AND 14 IN BREADTH AND 12 IN HEIGHT.' (GILPIN'S *MEMOIR*)

his *Lakes* account to show this. The artist where necessary should be prepared to add or subtract a detail - 'trees he may generally plant or remove at pleasure', wrote Gilpin. A 'withered stump' might replace the spreading oak, or indeed, vice versa, if the picturesque character of the whole would be thereby enhanced.[16]

One famous writer who appreciated Gilpin's *Tours* was Jane Austen, as attested by her brother Henry[17] and also, as clearly shown in her novels, where a reference often adds delight to her irony. To take just two examples: in *Northanger Abbey*, Henry Tilney instructs Catherine Morland in the Picturesque and she is 'so hopeful a scholar that when they gained the top of Beechen Cliff she voluntarily rejected the whole city of Bath as unworthy to make part of a landscape'.[18] In *Pride and Prejudice* we have a scene at Netherfield where Elizabeth Bennet provides a very nice touch. She is walking with Mrs Hurst in the shrubbery and they unexpectedly meet Darcy and Miss Bingley. Mrs Hurst takes Mr Darcy's disengaged arm, rudely leaving Elizabeth to walk by herself. Darcy immediately says, 'The walk is not wide enough for our party. We had better go into the avenue.' But Elizabeth laughingly answers, 'No, no, stay where you are. You are charmingly grouped and appear to uncommon advantage. The picturesque would be spoilt by admitting a fourth. Goodbye.'[19]

Theorising on the picturesque continued in the publications of other writers such as Uvedale Price but perhaps the best example of Gilpin's extraordinary reach into the general public's consciousness was his rapid identification with Thomas Rowlandson's and William Combe's caricature in their *Tour of Dr Syntax in Search of the Picturesque*.[20] Published in 1809, it tells of a penurious schoolmaster-curate who sets off on his horse, Grizzle, 'to make a Tour and work it up'.

> I'll ride and write and sketch and print   And thus create a real mint

He loses his way; the sign-post is illegible, so he waits for a passer-by as guide

> Upon that bank awhile I'll sit       And let poor Grizzle graze a bit
> And so my time shall not be lost     I'll make a drawing of the post
> And though a flimsy taste shall flout it
> There's something picturesque about it
> Tis rude and rough without a gloss
> And is well covered o'er with moss
> And I've a right - who dares deny it?
> To place yon group of asses by it . . .
> I'll make this flat a shaggy ridge   And o'er the water throw a bridge . . .
> And though from truth I haply err
> 'The scene preserves its character'

- and thus Combe makes fun of Gilpin's 'picturesque' precepts. Some of his verses would have hurt this kindly, modest man had he been alive, particularly those linking him to a typical virago-like wife, but there is no doubt of their entertainment value and the cleverness of Rowlandson's drawings.

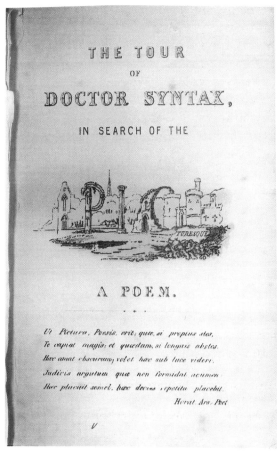

THE TOUR
OF
DOCTOR SYNTAX,
IN SEARCH OF THE

*PIC*

*TURESQUE*

A POEM.

. . .

*Ut Pictura, Poesis, erit; quæ, si propius stes,*
*Te capiat magis; et quædam, si longius abstes.*
*Hæc amat obscurum; volet hæc sub luce videri,*
*Judicis argutum quæ non formidat acumen*
*Hæc placuit semel, hæc decies repetita placebit.*

*Horat. Ars. Poet*

*v*

FRONTISPIECE TO THE 1868 EDITION
(LONDON, J.C. HOTTEN, PICCADILLY)

It would be wrong, however, to conclude this introduction to Gilpin's life and writings on the Picturesque without mentioning a major gift he possessed which makes those remarks of his that were an easy target for the humourists, fade into insignificance; and that is his transcendent visionary power. It is of a kind which anticipates Wordsworth's 'inner eye'. Writing about the beauty of Nature, he says it 'strikes us beyond the power of thought . . . every mental operation is suspended' and the soul melts.[21] It is but a step from that to the great poetry of *Tintern Abbey*.

But now to return to 1768 and Gilpin's local Surrey tour and to see what became of those landmarks that interested him as he journeyed towards 'Rygate' and Dorking.

NOTES TO CHAPTER I

Much of the information in this chapter has been drawn direct from Gilpin's *Memoirs of Dr Richard Gilpin and of his Posterity* which also includes 'An Account of the Author by Himself'. Edited by William Jackson, it was published on behalf of the Cumberland and Westmoreland Antiquarian and Archaeological Society in 1879. Detailed references are not provided where this is the source.

1   Bodleian Library, Oxford, MSS. Eng. misc. c. 389-90, letter of 21 May 1790. Mary Hartley, the daughter of David Hartley, the philosopher, was a gifted amateur artist

who first heard of Gilpin in 1780 when visiting the poet and writer William Mason. She met Gilpin briefly only once, in the following year, and then corresponded regularly with him, chiefly on matters of the picturesque, until her death in 1803.

2  *Observations on Several Parts of England, particularly the Mountains and Lakes of Cumberland and Westmoreland* . . . (1786), vol. 1, section ix.

3  Letter to Sir George Beaumont, 21 July 1802, quoted by C P Barbier, *William Gilpin, His Drawings, Teaching and Theory of the Picturesque* (Oxford, 1963).

4  Anthonie Waterloo (*c.* 1610-76), native of Lille, best known for his landscape engravings. His prints were much admired by Gilpin - 'a name above any other in landscape' - *Essay on Prints* (1798), p. 149.

5  Bodleian Library, Oxford, MS. Eng. misc. b. 73, letter of 10 October 1742.

6  Gilpin's sixteenth century forebear, a follower of Erasmus and fearless preacher who refused the Bishopric of Carlisle and became Rector of Houghton-le-Spring, a wild parish. He died in 1584.

7  That William Gilpin was the author of the *Dialogue* was established by William Templeman, *Life and Work of William Gilpin* (University of Illinois, 1939), p. 34.

8  The complete text of the *Dialogue* is not easy to come by; there are generous extracts, including Polyphon's comment, in John Dixon Hunt and Peter Willis, *The Genius of the Place* (MIT Press, 1975, revised edition 1988), pp. 254-9.

9  The Sanxays were originally Huguenots; James' grandfather had come over from France at the time of the revocation of the Edict of Nantes (1685). See Edward Peel, *Cheam School from 1645* (Thornhill Press, 1975), pp. 26-7.

10 It is likely, however, that the London school had joined with the school in Cheam, which was already well-established at and probably near Whitehall (Edward Peel, as above). In 1719, it moved to the site of what is now Tabor Court at the top of Cheam High Street, remaining there for over two hundred years. The Duke of Edinburgh was a pupil from 1930-3 just before the school moved to Berkshire in 1934. It has since amalgamated with Hawtreys School and flourishes as Cheam-Hawtreys Preparatory School.

11 Dr Joseph Warton was from 1766-93 a 'conspicuously unsuccessful' headmaster of Winchester College, though a distinguished man of letters. His behaviour was somewhat eccentric, his discipline poor and bullying among the boys was rife; see Peter Virgin, *Sydney Smith* (HarperCollins, 1994), ch. 2.

12 There could have been contributory reasons; see Philip Ziegler, *Addington* (Collins, 1965).

13 As well as Gilpin's account in his memoir, see also his Introduction to the *Lakes Tour*. He dedicated the book to Queen Charlotte.

14 William Sawrey Gilpin (1762-1843) was the first President of the Watercolour Society (formed in 1804), but, in fact, seems to have been more successful finally as a landscape gardener than as a painter.

15 His wife survived him for just over three years. 'One grave in Boldre churchyard contains the mortal remains of this exemplary pair.' Ed. note at the close of Gilpin's *Memoir*.

16 See Gilpin's *Lakes Tour*, vol. 1, section xxviii and Essay III on 'The Art of Sketching Landscape' in *Three Essays* (1791).

17 'At a very early age she was enamoured of Gilpin on the Picturesque' - Henry Austen in his Biographical Notice to *Northanger Abbey* and *Persuasion*; R. W. Chapman (ed.), *The Novels of Jane Austen*, (6 vols., OUP, 1923-54), vol. 5. See also Mavis Batey, *Jane Austen and the English Landscape* (Barn Elms, 1996).

18 *Northanger Abbey*, ch. 14.
19 *Pride and Prejudice*, ch. 10.
20 Two more *Tours of Dr Syntax* followed and the three were published together in 1812. Rowlandson executed the coloured plates and drawings and Combe then composed the accompanying verses. A small exhibition at Cheam's Whitehall includes some of Rowlandson's *Syntax* drawings and later ceramics, including lustreware, decorated with Dr Syntax scenes.
21 *Three Essays*: Essay II on 'Picturesque Travel'.

DR SYNTAX LOSING HIS WAY.

. . . AS HE PONDERED WHAT TO DO
A GUIDE-POST ROSE WITHIN HIS VIEW

EXTRACT FROM JOHN ROCQUE, *MAP OF SURREY* (1768)
POTTER'S LANE IS MARKED AT LOWER CENTRE

14

## CHAPTER II - CHEAM TO REIGATE

'*Over the Downs to Potter's Lane is about three miles. The Downs afford no great variety. The ground in many parts is beautifully laid out; the furzy part contrasts with the smooth; the eye is in many places agreeably entertained with winding roads, traversing the heath in various directions; and the edge of the whole is pleasantly skirted with wood; among which the spire of Bansted is an object. At the entrance of Potter's Lane, if you turn round, you have a view nobly extensive. The distant parts of it melt entirely into an ocean of air. From that downy height you are considerably raised above the country, and have a stretch of many leagues before you. The parts are pleasantly blended; but not enough separated. You do not see that pleasing difference between wood and plain, which is so agreeable in a landskip; and which catches large bodies of light:* Late discriminat agros.[\*] *There is a want too of objects. St Paul's is a very fine one; but there is nothing else of use in the way, except Wimbledon-house; and that only when the sun shines upon it. Indeed St Paul's and Wimbledon are both too insignificant. In such an expanse as this there should be several objects; and at different distances, some within three, four or five miles of the eye which would give them strength, and consequence in the landskip. These are removed 14 or 15 miles. In short, the beauty of the view consists principally in its vastness, and in the agreeable contrast it makes with the smooth surface of the Downs.*

'*As you go up Potter's Lane, you have catches of the same country, on the left; which being seen through the hedge-row trees, and having the advantage of foreground, appear to more advantage.*

'*On the entrance of Walton-heath you have a wild and desolate view. Nothing can be more dreary, and comfortless. Nor is there the least catch of distant country to shew you that you are in a cultivated land. A solitary*

---

[\*]Virgil, *Aeneid*, Book XI, 144, describing how the flames from the Arcadians lighted the road and 'far and wide threw up the outlines of the field'.

*wind-mill, and a spire, on the right, just tell you that the country is inhabited. In a mile's riding you come to a dip in the heath, which lets in a little of the country, and adds some variety.*

*'At the turnpike, which is about 4 miles from Ryegate, you get into an open lane, which is not unpleasant. The views towards Gatton, on the left, serve you to range over, till that vast expanse of country breaks in upon you, from the top of Ryegate-hill. The parts are in general larger, than the view from Potter's Lane; and in some places the distance is very picturesque.'*

## BANSTEAD DOWNS

WILLIAM Gilpin left Cheam for his August day's excursion on a circular route of about 27 miles, stopping at Dorking for 'a dish of tea' and having just time to examine the main features of the Rookery at Westcott before he set back. Over the Banstead Downs his way lay south to Reigate Hill and, as with the rest of his journey, John Rocque's map[1] surveyed about 1760 is very helpful in indicating his route.

He busies himself jotting down his reactions to the type of terrain he crosses, observing the woodland that skirted the whole and the spire of Banstead Church above the trees; these features provided interest and definition even if the area lacked real variety. From Gilpin's comments the reader gains an insight into what is needed to make the whole 'picturesque'. Not only is variety required, particularly of light and shade, with plenty of light catching the different types of countryside, but 'objects' at the appropriate distance 'to give them consequence'. Both St Paul's and Wimbledon House are too far off to make a focus for the eye. Further, when he enters Potter's Lane, he records its advantage in that here are breaks in the hedgerows so that, as one passes by, the trees act as a frame for glimpses of the country, thus making a suitable foreground for a picture.

Not that he is insensible to pure beauty. It is interesting to note that in writing of the 'nobly extensive' view from the Downs, Gilpin corrects his first manuscript version that 'the distant parts of it are entirely lost in air' to the much more evocative 'melt entirely into an ocean of air'. Throughout his writings he was at pains to distinguish between the quality of beauty as such and the picturesque.

Banstead Downs, the name often used imprecisely over the neighbouring downland area, was already famed. John Aubrey,[2] who visited Banstead in 1692, writes of 'the wholsom air' of the district, 'formerly much

16

prescribed by the London physicians to their patients', and adds that it is well known for 'its small, sweet mutton' - the source of wealth to the local farmers since mediaeval times - and its races. 'Here is a horse race much frequented, a four mile course', he says.[3] Samuel Pepys in 1663 had written of 'a great thronging to Bansted Downs upon a great horse-race and foot-race' which he wished he could have attended.[4]

BANSTEAD DOWNS FROM *VILLAGE LONDON* BY EDWARD WALFORD
(FIRST PUBLISHED IN 1883/4)

This prized open space was almost entirely lost, together with the other Commons, at the end of the nineteenth century. They were threatened by Sir John Hartopp who saw, particularly in Banstead Downs, an ideal area for building development. He bought the Lordship of the Manor in 1873 and began on his schemes to take over the ancient rights of the commoners. He was eventually foiled but not until after a long, costly legal struggle by the local inhabitants. Because of their determination and some influential support, the downland is in large part still an amenity today.[5]

As for the 'objects' William Gilpin speaks of, Banstead's All Saints' Church, though now hidden from view, still boasts its spire on the top of its thirteenth century tower, the rest of the building dating back to the late twelfth century. Aubrey records that at the west end of the church was 'a spire made of slates' with its cross on the top,[6] and gives an account of the

17

monuments within the church. Over the years, there has been much restoration and various additions but it is worth mentioning the Pre-Raphaelite stained glass west window installed in 1892.[7]

*BANSTEAD CHURCH*, WATERCOLOUR ON PENCIL BY JOHN HASSELL (1823)

Of the two other 'objects', Wren's 'very fine' St Paul's needs no comment but the distant Wimbledon House, long destroyed, is a less obvious reference. It was completed by 1733 for Sarah, Duchess of Marlborough (1660-1744), not without recrimination and difficulty, a fine Palladian mansion of grey brick, facing south. Once the sun shone on it, it would, as Gilpin says, be visible from the 'downy height' of Banstead. It was burnt down in 1785 in the time of her descendants, the Spencers, and the ground was cleared and levelled. Today the area is part of the playing field of Park House Middle School, just off Wimbledon's Arthur Road.[8]

Potter's Lane, which Gilpin next rode along, was originally part of the Brighton Road, the modern A217, which had its beginnings in 1755. In 1826, the line of the road was altered so that it took a more direct course but the path of the original lane can still be detected, behind the gardens of Green Curve, from a point just west of the traffic lights at the junction with Fir Tree Road, to emerge on to the A217 on the Sutton side of Burgh Wood road. Potter as a surname seems to have derived from the Cheam Potteries which flourished in mediaeval times, dwindling in importance by the seventeenth century.[9]

ON entering Walton Heath, William Gilpin is struck by the 'wild and desolate view . . .'

Nothing picturesque here; only the windmill and a church spire in the distance suggest that there are even any inhabitants and he moves on towards Gatton. Had he passed nearer to the windmill, he would certainly have enjoyed a more picturesque sight than the remaining mill body, seen between the trees on the edge of Banstead Heath. A black post mill, sailless, it

EXTRACT FROM JOHN ROCQUE, *MAP OF SURREY* (1768)

*WALTON HEATH*, ETCHING BY PERCY ROBERTSON SHOWING TADWORTH [WALTON] MILL

19

stands in the garden of a house now used as offices just beyond Mill Road in Tadworth and is valued for being the only known surviving mill in Surrey with a two-storeyed roundhouse. It was last worked in 1902, the site holding two mills at least from the late eighteenth century until 1890; documentary evidence showing that mills have been there for centuries. The attractive etching by Percy Robertson, held by the Victoria and Albert Museum with the title *Walton Heath* (1913), shows the windmill with four sails, but it has been suggested that, for the sake of pictorial quality, it was drawn with its full complement, two of the sails having, in fact, dropped off in 1893 and the mill worked by a steam engine.[10]

St. Peter's, Walton on the Hill, in the eighteenth century, showing its original shingled spire

The spire in the distance was that of St Peter's at Walton on the Hill. Like Banstead's church spire, it was originally shingled. Aubrey deplores the state of the church windows which had been of good painted glass, now 'much abus'd by Fanatick Rage; so that but little remains'.[11] The interior and its memorials are also described and particular mention made of the twelfth century font, which is in fact earlier than the church: 'At the West end, a little Northward, is a very old leaden Fount, adorn'd with nine Figures in a sitting posture, their Faces much mangled'.[12] Considered a small but remarkable work, it is today thought to be the oldest surviving lead font in Britain. The church itself has undergone much renewal. By 1820 the tower supporting the spire required considerable strengthening. The spire was removed and the tower top ornamented with pinnacles which themselves proved too heavy and in 1895 a lower square-shaped tower was built which remains today.[13]

Most people know of Walton Heath because of its now famous golf course. Opened in May 1904, it has since hosted European Championships and the Ryder Cup and the area is far removed from the uninhabited appearance that Gilpin noted as he passed by.

A DETAIL FROM THE LEAD FONT
AT ST. PETER'S, WALTON ON THE HILL.
AUBREY'S 'MANGLED' FACES CANNOT BE MISSED

WALTON UPON HILL CHURCH, N. W., WITH ITS PINNACLES,
ENGRAVED BY P. SIMONAU (UNDATED BUT AFTER 1820)

21

I T is almost impossible to discount the presence of the motorway to share Gilpin's experience of the pleasant scenes towards Gatton and to let your eye 'range over' them, but draw into the National Trust car-park on Reigate Hill and the vast expanse of country to the south 'breaks in upon you' just as he says. Views to the South Downs on a clear day are magnificent, as are those nearer to Leith and Box Hills, gained by walking a little further westwards. Although William Gilpin's objective was the Rookery and he mentions Gatton just in passing, it certainly should not be missed on a present-day itinerary. Before commenting on the first notable development of the grounds, it is worth recalling that Gatton was already notoriously a 'rotten borough'. Two members of Parliament represented it, the power of election residing in the Lords of the Manor of Gatton and of Upper Gatton respectively. In fact, three years

GATTON 'TOWN HALL'

before Gilpin rode past, with what Pevsner terms 'urbane irony', a so-called 'Town Hall' - an open Doric temple - had been built on a knoll in the park. This is still in existence and well worth a visit.

Today Gatton is divided into two areas. The western park of over 200 acres belongs to the National Trust, about half presented by the then owners, the Colman family, in 1952, and the rest bought with donated funds three years later. Although the eastern part, of similar extent, is private and, with the house, now forms the Royal Alexandra and Albert School complex, its impressive and historic grounds are open at regular times during the summer months.

In 1768, 'Capability' Brown,[14] so-called because of his habit of speaking of the 'capabilities' for improvement of any given landscape, was already carrying out work for Sir George Colebrook, the owner of Gatton since 1761. Brown had received the substantial sum of £3,055, as detailed in the notebook held in the Royal Horticultural Society's Lindley Library, and was constructing the Great Water, the long curving lake which is Gatton's most striking feature. He added cedars to the wood north of the lake and planted the lakeside drive with trees, these being placed alternately by the waterside and on the edge of the fields or woods, thus revealing in turns lake views and hinterland. Throughout the remaining grassland, groups of trees were scattered in his calculatedly 'random' fashion.

In order to buy this desirable estate from his nieces, Sir George had sold many of his other properties. Even so, after only ten years at Gatton, he went bankrupt and was compelled to relinquish the land he had so wanted. However, he was subsequently employed as secretary to the Bank of England, so presumably managed to live at a tolerable standard even if he lost Gatton.

After Sir George Colebrook, there was a series of short ownerships, including that of Sir Robert Ladbroke, who kindly compensated the incumbent vicar of Gatton Church for the church lands which Brown's great lake had swallowed up. In 1798, the estate was bought by Sir Mark Wood,[15] newly retired from service in India, who was said at one time to have gambled Gatton on the races, a bet he presumably must have won. He made few alterations to the estate. There are attractive watercolours by John Hassell of the house and other buildings in the park, as for example, the 'Castle' in Sir Mark's time and Kew Lodge.

LOWER GATTON HOUSE, SEAT OF SIR WILLIAM (MARK) WOOD.
WATERCOLOUR ON PENCIL BY JOHN HASSELL (1822)

| Nº | Names of Inclosed Lands &c | Grass &c A R P | | | Arable A R P | | | Woodland A R P | | |
|----|------------------------------|-----|---|---|---|---|---|---|---|---|
| | The Park as in the Plan | 376 | 0 | 3 | 131 | 0 | 3 | 75 | 0 | 25 |
| | | 131 | 0 | 3 | | | | | | |
| | | 75 | 0 | 25 | | | | | | |
| | | 582 | 0 | 31 | | | | | | |
| | **The Constituant Parts** | | | | | | | | | |
| | The Mansion & Offices Pleasure Ground Old & New Kitchen Gardens Stables Barns Yards & the Carpenters house, Yard & Orchard | 24 | 1 | 4 | | | | | | |
| | The Ponds | 34 | 2 | 0 | | | | | | |
| 1 | Pheasentry | 4 | 1 | 39 | | | | | | |
| 2 | Nutwood | 10 | 1 | 14 | | | | | | |
| 3 | Buckwood | 13 | 1 | 35 | | | | | | |
| 4 | Coven Hill & Plantation on the East Side of the Quarry | 13 | 3 | 24 | | | | | | |
| | The Remainder of the Park not Devided into Fields & Colᵈ Green | 260 | 0 | 22 | | | | | | |
| 5 | Quarry Field | 22 | 3 | 18 | | | | | | |
| 6 | West Hale | 15 | 1 | 24 | | | | | | |
| 7 | Oddy Croft | 11 | 0 | 5 | | | | | | |
| 8 | Gatton Grove | 10 | 0 | 0 | | | | | | |
| 9 | Below Gatton Grove | 10 | 0 | 19 | | | | | | |
| 10 | Hop Garden Field | 4 | 2 | 17 | | | | | | |
| 11 | & Lost Field | 2 | 3 | 3 | | | | | | |
| 12 | Seven Acres | 8 | 0 | 34 | | | | | | |
| 13 | | 4 | 2 | 6 | | | | | | |
| 14 | | 7 | 0 | 11 | | | | | | |
| 15 | | 4 | 0 | 5 | | | | | | |
| 16 | | 4 | 1 | 35 | | | | | | |
| 17 | | 5 | 1 | 0 | | | | | | |
| 18 | | 3 | 3 | 22 | | | | | | |
| 19 | | 7 | 2 | 22 | | | | | | |
| | **Taken in when last Paid** | | | | | | | | | |
| | Part of Barrow Field | 0 | 0 | 33 | | | | | | |
| | of Battle Bridge Field | 0 | 0 | 5 | | | | | | |
| | of Little Mead | 0 | 0 | 12 | | | | | | |
| | of Sandpit Field | 0 | 2 | 32 | | | | | | |
| | of Lower Rushouts | 0 | 1 | 12 | | | | | | |
| | | 582 | 0 | 31 | | | | | | |

SURVEY OF LOWER GATTON, C. 1790

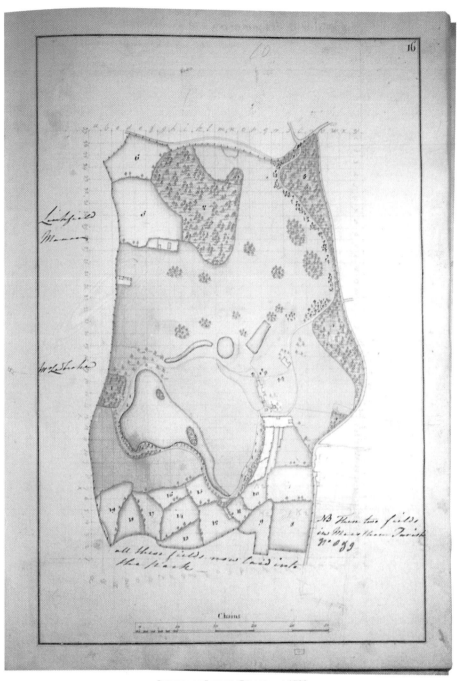

SURVEY OF LOWER GATTON, *c.* 1790

In 1830, Gatton was bought by the fifth Lord Monson, his main interest centring on the house, within which he created a unique and spectacular Marble Hall. It was completed on his death in 1841 by the sixth Lord who filled the entire house with what Burke in his *Visitation of the seats . . . of the noblemen and gentlemen of Great Britain* (1852-5) called 'every conceivable type of trophy: pictures, mirrors, fine furniture and carpets mostly obtained on the continent'. Nor did he neglect the grounds. William Keane[16] in 1849

THE CASTLE IN GATTON PARK, SEAT OF SIR MARK WOOD.
WATERCOLOUR ON PENCIL BY JOHN HASSELL (1822)

described the pleasure area of five acres as being 'divided into four quarters by broad gravel walks radiating from a fountain vase in the centre, bounded on the south by a terrace, commanding an extensive view of the splendid lake . . .' With its encroachment into Brown's carefully planned 'natural' landscape, the creation of this parterre echoes an important change in garden fashion.

In 1888, Gatton acquired its last private owner, Sir Jeremiah Colman, a philanthropist, a man of wide interests and apparently unflagging energy who, as well as heading the Colman family mustard firm, was high Sheriff to the county in the 1890s and a skilful and passionate orchid grower. For his work in orchid hybridisation, he was awarded in 1909 the Victoria Medal of Honour, the highest honour that the Royal Horticultural Society confers. Further pleasure grounds were laid out to the west of the house with winding paths punctuated by groups of trees and beds of shrubs. Individual small

*KEW LODGE, GATTON PARK.* WATERCOLOUR ON PENCIL BY JOHN HASSELL (1822)

gardens, such as a 'Japanese' garden and an 'Italian' garden as was the contemporary trend, were also created. The kitchen gardens with their walls of Reigate stone were carefully maintained and the orchid houses multiplied.

After a disastrous fire in 1934, the house had to be rebuilt. The Colmans moved away, though keeping the estate. Sir Jeremiah died in 1942 and, in due course, the estate was divided as already mentioned. In the 1990s there have been promising developments towards the regeneration of the School's acreage which contains so much historically interesting gardenland. A detailed survey was completed in 1997 by Cazenove Architects' Co-operative after full consultation with the School who have now embarked on an urgently needed restoration of the grounds and gardens. Between their care and that of the National Trust, Gatton is in good hands.

## NOTES TO CHAPTER II

1   John Rocque (1704/5-1762), a Huguenot whose family came to England *c.* 1709 and who became one of the most notable cartographers of the eighteenth century. Especially known for an outstanding map of London, he produced county, estate and further town maps which continued to be updated and issued by his publishing house, led by his wife after his death. The first Surrey map appeared in 1768.

2   John Aubrey (1626-1697), antiquary and biographer. Only his *Miscellanies* was published in his life-time. He toured Surrey in 1673, making further excursions in 1692 and his

*Perambulation of Surrey* was edited with additions by Rawlinson and published in 1719. This explains why some of the information goes beyond 1697. The work was reprinted by Kohler and Coombs, Dorking, and is available in most main libraries under the title *The Natural History and Antiquities of Surrey*.

3   Aubrey, vol. 2, pp. 96-8.

4   Robert Latham and William Matthews (eds.), *The Diary of Samuel Pepys* (London, 1971), vol. 4, 27 May 1663, p. 160.

5   For a full and interesting account see The Banstead History Research Group, *Banstead, a History* (1993), appendix A, p. 147.

6   Aubrey, vol. 2, p. 99. Presumably what Aubrey saw were shingles, i.e thin pieces of wood (oak) in the shape of tiles or slates, used for roofing. The *Surrey* volume in the Pevsner *Buildings of England* series (revised edition 1971) comments on the Surrey feature of 'shingling' (p. 82 and description of Burstow); Walton on the Hill church had the same finish on its (now vanished) spire.

7   A. Charles Sewter, *The Stained Glass of William Morris and his Circle* (Yale University Press, 1974), and its following *Catalogue* (1975). The window was produced in William Morris's workshop and shows, to the left, Ezekiel from a design by Dante Gabriel Rossetti, and, to the right, St John the Baptist by William Morris himself. Architectural canopies provided by Philip Webb.

8   See Richard Milward, *A Georgian Village, Wimbledon* (Wimbledon Society publication, 1986).

9   See A. J. Totman, *A History of the Manor and Parish of Burgh* (published by the author, 1970), p. 15 and Patricia Jackson, *Whitehall and Cheam Village* (London Borough of Sutton), pp. 18-9, which also shows a typical Cheamware jug.

10  Post mills were one of the earliest types of windmills, where the mill-body rotates by pivoting on a central (usually oak) post. They were mounted on roundhouses, with one or more storeys, serving generally as storerooms. Outwood is a fine example. For details see K. G. Farries and M. T. Mason, *The Windmills of Surrey and Inner London* (Charles Skilton Ltd., London, 1966).

11  Aubrey, vol. 2, p 287.

12  Ibid., p. 290.

13  Walton on the Hill Local History Society, *Newsletter* no. 12 (Summer 1994).

14  Lancelot (Capability) Brown (1716-83) was the leading landscape designer from the 1750s until his death. His formation of large and beautiful lakes amid parkland studded with clumps of trees was his hall-mark - thereby he often demolished formal gardens and venerable old tree-lined avenues. Gilpin was, on the whole, an admirer of his work but critical of the sometimes unnatural boundaries in his stretches of 'made' water.

15  Sir Mark Wood (1747-1829) had a distinguished career in Bengal but retired to England in 1793 on health grounds. He became an MP the following year, lost his seat (Shaftesbury) in 1802 but, having acquired Gatton with its 'rotten' borough, remained an MP until 1818 when he retired from public life. He was buried in Gatton church.

16  William Keane in his *Beauties of Surrey being a particular description of about one hundred and twenty seats of the nobility and gentry in the county of Surrey . . . ,* (London, 1849 ?), gives much interesting detail of the notable parks and gardens of Surrey.

Information about the division of Gatton kindly supplied by the National Trust (Southern Region) and of the Colman family through the kindness of Unilever Archives, Port Sunlight.

# CHAPTER III - REIGATE TO DORKING

'*From Ryegate towards Dorking you pass over a common about half a mile; at the close of which you have a picturesque view. A good foreground of trees, and broken ground, with a winding road, a first distance of woody hedgerows well grouped and shapen; beyond them a second distance of rising ground. From hence you enter into a close lane; some part of it very close, rocky on each side, over-hung thick with wood, dark and gloomy. In many parts you have agreeable catches of hilly ground, which in some places appear to great advantage over trees. On the left Beachworth-castle, rising among wood, makes a beautiful object, and puts you in mind of Poussin. Another view of it presents itself, through an opening of the hedge, still more picturesque than the last; only it is in some degree hurt by the regularity of a row of trees, which should be cut up, or broken, to make the view quite agreeable.*

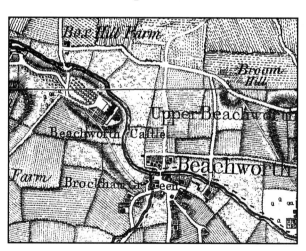

GILPIN'S REIGATE ROAD, PART OF WHICH STILL RUNS TO BOX HILL FARM AND THEN DROPS DOWN TO CROSS THE MOLE, CAN BE SEEN IN THE UPPER SECTION OF ROCQUE'S MAP

'*Over the bridge over the Mole, the view is pleasant. The river forms a little contracted bay, shadowed round with wood. Beyond appears at a distance on an eminence Mr King's house, (formerly Tyre's) which at that distance has the appearance of a castle. The landscape is such as would suit Berghem's pencil. Fill the water with cattle coolling [sic] their toes; place a shepherd on the shore with a female peasant, a dog, and 2 or 3 cows; give the sky a glow, and you have one of his pictures.*'

29

PAUSING at the end of Reigate Common, Gilpin considers the features of the scene before him, his picture-making eye enjoying the foreground of trees, broken surfaces and winding road, and the middle distance with its woods and well-placed hedgerows completed by the hills rising behind. He proceeds next through an overhung, somewhat closed-in lane,[1] but is rewarded by glimpses of the country to the south and, rising out of the woods on the far side of the Mole Valley, by the sight of

VIEW OF BETCHWORTH CASTLE, SOMETIME BEFORE 1737.[2]
THIS PICTURE WELL ILLUSTRATES THE PRE-EMINENCE OF THE SITE

Beachworth (Betchworth) Castle. He is at once reminded of Poussin and, with landscape artists very much in mind, he arrives at the bridge over the river. On a hill in the distance 'Mr King's house' is clearly discernible, the whole rural landscape being 'such as would suit Berghem's pencil'. Gaspard Poussin (1615-75) adopted the surname of his brother-in-law and teacher, Nicolas Poussin, and, with Claude and Salvator Rosa, was one of the most collected and imitated landscape painters of the age. Nicolaes Berchem (1720-83) was also very popular and, a master of etching, he made his own and many other artists' pictures available as prints. Both specialised in

NICOLAES BERCHEM, *ITALIAN LANDSCAPE WITH PEASANTS AND CATTLE,*, WATERCOLOUR DRAWING.
'FILL THE WATER WITH CATTLE COOLING THEIR TOES; PLACE A SHEPHERD ON THE SHORE . . .'

idealised, Italianate compositions, Poussin preferring a more classical form, Berchem particularly enjoying the pastoral with its grazing animals. Gilpin had a large collection of his prints, as he stated in his *Essay* of 1753. 'His execution is inimitable', he adds. 'His cattle . . . are well-drawn, admirably characterised and generally well-grouped.'[3]

*THE EAST VIEW OF BETCHWORTH CASTLE,* SHOWING THE 'VENETIAN WINDOW' LAKE. S .& N. BUCK (1737)

31

The Betchworth Castle that Gilpin saw belonged to Abraham Tucker.[4] Much of the original mediaeval castle had been pulled down by the previous owner who rebuilt it as a fine castellated country house. Tucker took a lively interest in his property, studying agriculture so that he could supervise his farms and visiting them on foot. His park was laid out in formal fashion with avenues of limes and elm (see map); he planted one, it is said, 280 yards long,[5] one lime avenue being in existence as late as the 1960s. The east front was ornamented with water-gardens, since completely obliterated. Nowadays there is a fishing lake, but originally the centre area was laid out in 'Venetian window' shape.[6] Abraham Tucker bequeathed Betchworth to his daughter. After her death in 1794, it was occupied and well managed by Henry Peters, of the banking family, but by 1834, somewhat neglected by his son, it was bought by Henry Thomas Hope of Deepdene to enlarge his estate. He dismantled the building, leaving it as a 'picturesque' ruin. What remains, which is now the subject of renewed interest, is still closed off.[7]

AN IMPRESSION OF PART OF THE
CASTLE RUINS IN THE 1960S

SIR JOHN SOANE'S STABLE BLOCK TODAY. IT WAS COMMISSIONED BY HENRY PETERS, A DIRECTOR
OF THE BANK OF ENGLAND, TO WHICH SOANE HAD BEEN APPOINTED ARCHITECT IN 1788

There are still many beautiful trees in the former park. In 1964 Abraham Tucker's remaining lime avenue was declared unsafe and felled but most of the replacement saplings now stand proud on the rise of the downland;[8] ancient oaks survive and there are remnants too of old sweet chestnuts. 'I have heard', writes Gilpin of Betchworth in his *Forest Scenery*, '... there are not fewer than seventy or eighty chestnuts measuring from twelve to eighteen or twenty feet in girth and some of them in very picturesque form'.[9] Today the largest remaining is about thirty-five feet round and Gilpin would find that and much of the surroundings composing a delightful picture. Since 1912, however, Betchworth Golf Club has had a course there and also, with no public access, Dorking Anglers manage the extended fishing lake just beyond. Sir John Soane's stable-block, now converted to housing is the only reminder of Betchworth Castle's happier architectural past.[10]

## DENBIES

JUST as altered as Betchworth, but welcoming the general public as a business, is Denbies, Gilpin's 'Mr King's house, formerly Tyre's'. Jonathan Tyers' story has often been recounted[11] as it was he who made the most extraordinary garden of the century. He had, in 1732, re-opened the pleasure garden at Vauxhall, which, with

DENBIES, ENGRAVED BY T. BARBER
FROM A DRAWING BY J.P. NEALE (1826)

its leafy avenues, the many decorative buildings, the statues of Milton and Handel, together with its ornamented supper boxes and its music, became one of the most visited places in London. Vauxhall was the realm of *L'Allegro*, Milton's Happy Man, a version of whose poem, together with its companion piece, *Il Penseroso*, Handel set to music in 1740. Denbies was to be the setting for the contemplative man. Tyers bought the land in 1734, rebuilt its farmhouse and developed the estate into an area for meditation and stark reminders of death. Beyond the entrance marked *'Procul este profani'*

*A General Prospect of Vauxhall Gardens*
*Shewing at one view the disposition of the whole Gardens . . .*

*The Triumphal Arches, Mr. Handel's Statue, Etc., in the South Walk of Vauxhall Gardens*

These two illustrations were engraved
by L.S. Muller from drawings by J. Wale
(Undated but *c.* 1750s)

(Stay far off, ye profane ones) were eight acres of woodland called *Il Penseroso*. Winding walks contained gloomy and macabre monuments and carved figures, inscriptions and poems, all relating to one's end. The Temple of Death included a memorial to the gifted Lord Petre[12] who had died at the untimely age of twenty-nine. A gate with stone coffins surmounted by skulls led to the Valley of the Shadow of Death where two paintings by Francis Hayman,[13] of life-sized figures, showed a calm Christian dying and the tortured ending of an unbeliever. Jonathan Tyers, who lived at his house in Vauxhall Gardens in the week, spent his Sundays at Denbies amid these solemn, indeed alarming, surroundings. He died in 1767 and the estate was bought by Gilpin's Mr King - the Hon. Peter King[14] - who straightaway removed all 'the eccentric imageries' as John Timbs puts it in his *Picturesque Promenade round Dorking*.[15]

*STEALING A KISS,* BY FRANCIS HAYMAN, FROM THE ORIGINAL PAINTING IN VAUXHALL GARDENS. ENGRAVING BY TRUCHY (DATE UNKNOWN)

Denbies passed through the hands of several owners before the best known, Thomas Cubitt,[16] purchased the estate. The Denisons (1787-1849), particularly, had enlarged the grounds and cared for the gardens. Thomas Cubitt, however, worked to a large scale. He had collaborated with Prince Albert in remodelling Osborne House and bought Denbies in 1850 and set about building a new mansion for himself and his family. He planted generously, ordering more than six thousand young pines and other trees,

35

together with rare plants and shrubs. His friendship with Joseph Hooker of Kew was a help in their selection. He also established a huge range of glasshouses. His son became the first Lord Ashcombe after serving in the House of Commons for over thirty years. Denbies continued in the family,[17] though with much loss of land caused by severe financial constraints, until the 1980s. Some of the estate was sold, some was passed by the Treasury to the National Trust in lieu of death duties. The third Lord Ashcombe, unable to sustain the upkeep of the mansion, converted the laundry and other subsidiary accommodation into a new house and the original building was eventually demolished. Henry Cubitt, the fourth Lord, sold the house and the remaining 635 acres in 1984 to Adrian White who has made it his family home. Two years later he planted the vineyard and, despite damage in the 1987 hurricane, it has flourished and the present Winery was opened to the public in 1993. Adrian White has preserved some of Thomas Cubitt's garden features and is well known as a local benefactor. What is more, like Charles Howard of Deepdene in the seventeenth century and Charles Hamilton at Painshill in the eighteenth, he has re-established a famed link with our distant occupiers, the Romans, who also had vineyards in the area.

*DENBIGHS, THE SEAT OF DENNISON, ESQ.*
WATERCOLOUR ON PENCIL BY JOHN HASSELL (UNDATED)

There are still the beautiful views across the valley, in which the traffic is hidden, to Box Hill and the North Downs, just of the kind that William Gilpin saw as he trotted along the old road to Mickleham. But first he was off to Dorking where, stopping at one of the several inns to hire a carriage, he set off for the Rookery.

1  A section of the Old Reigate Road leading to Box Hill Farm. It is still possible to see from here across the valley to the site of Betchworth Castle. Part of the farm is now National Trust property.

2  The following note appears on this painting: 'Betchworth Castle from a painting in the possession of W. Peters ... Copied from an old painting in the hall of the castle which must have been drawn before 1737, the date of [the] Bucks' engraving.'

3  *Essay on Prints* (2nd edition, 1798), p. 129.

4  Abraham Tucker (1705-1774), a humane and cultivated man, wrote a long philosophical work, *The Light of Nature Pursued*, for which he was well known at the time. He added Chart Farm and land to his possessions but re-sold it in 1759 (see the Rookery).

5  J. S. Bright, *A History of Dorking* (1884), p. 159.

6  S. and N. Buck, *Buck's Antiquities or memorable remains of above four hundred castles, monasteries, palaces, etc., etc. in England and Wales* ... (London, 1774), vol. 2, pl. 277. This attractive engraving, dated 25 March 1737, is dedicated to Abraham Tucker. 'Situate on a fine eminence' the east view of Betchworh Castle includes the 'Venetian' lake with its fountain and the formal tree planting below the house.

7  Mole Valley District Council has recently (October 2000) commissioned a Conservation Plan for Betchworth Castle. This has been prepared in draft form for public consultation by Broadway Malyon Cultural Heritage of Weybridge, Surrey. It has much interesting detail of the original buildings and the estate.

8  Surrey County Council holds photographs, taken in February 1962, which give an idea of how impressive the original avenues must have been.

9  *Forest Scenery*, vol. 1, p. 129.

10  Constructed in 1799.

11  An excellent account is that by Brian Allen, 'Jonathan Tyers's Other Garden', *Journal of Garden History*, vol. 1, no. 3, (1981), pp. 215-38. See also the *Gentleman's Magazine*, vol. 51, p. 123.

12  Lord Petre (1713-42) was one of the leading botanists and gardeners of his generation. From 1732, he planned the notable grounds of Thorndon Hall in Essex. Peter Collinson, a friend and well-known naturalist, wrote of his early death as 'the greatest loss that gardening or botany ever felt in this island'. Miles Hadfield, *A History of British Gardening* (Penguin, 1985), p. 226.

13  Francis Hayman (1708-78) had already provided paintings for the supper-boxes at Vauxhall, on which his fame still rests.

14  Of the well-known Surrey family. They were Barons of Ockham. The first Lord King (1669-1734) became Lord Chancellor in 1725. There is 'a fine portrait' monument to him, as Pevsner says, in Ockham Church. The Hon. Peter King became sixth baron in 1779 and re-sold Denbies in 1781, keeping the land that adjoined the Ockham estates.

15  *A Picturesque Promenade round Dorking* (1823), p. 49.

16  Hermione Hobhouse, *Thomas Cubitt, Master Builder* (1971), p. 465 ff.

17  S.E.D. Fortescue, *The House on the Hill* (1993), published and distributed by the Denbies Wine Estate, gives an interesting and full account of the development of Denbies to the present time.

EXTRACT FROM LINDLEY & CROSLEY, *MAP OF SURREY*, FIRST PUBLISHED 1793.
THE ROOKERY IS MARKED AT LOWER LEFT AND DENBIES, THE DEEPDENE AND
NORBURY PARK ARE ALSO SHOWN

# CHAPTER IV - THE ROOKERY

*THE ROOKERY, SEAT OF R. FULLER,* WATERCOLOUR ON PENCIL BY JOHN HASSELL (1823)

*'At Dorking I swallowed a dish of tea, and got into a chaise for the Rookery, leaving my horse to bait.*

*The late proprietor of the place, Mr Malthouse, found, I was told, a mere wilderness. The ground-plot is a valley between two woody hills. Part of the valley was watery. The hills were a thicket; and the water a bed of sedge. He has literally done nothing but remove deformities, and add variety. The water he has cleared, and formed into a lake: the woods he has opened in many places; and exhibited a variety of lawns, open groves, and close recesses. Everything is grand, simple, and uniform; the purest nature I ever met with in any improvement. At Stow, at Kew, at Painshill, you see the greatest profusion of expence. You every where see the hand of art: Nature never makes her excursions in such polished walks; plants her shrubberies, and her ever-greens in such artificial combinations; and brings vistas, and* objects together with so much forced antithesis. But in all the beautiful sylvan scenes here exhibited nothing is introduced, but what nature herself might be supposed to create. Where you have a barren spot to improve, you must do the best you can: but certainly the simple scenes of pure nature have something ravishing in them, which art can never produce.

It would require long examination to criticise particularly each of the beautiful scenes here exhibited. Those which struck me most were the following.

The lake is one. It covers, I should imagine, about half a dozen acres. The water, surrounded on every side by hanging woods, rising from the very edge, doubles a promontary of beach, and alders, opens in a second bay upon an island, on which stands a temple dedicated to Venus. The whole scene is a noble amphitheatre, and infinitely pleasing. Such a piece of simple nature far excells any made water, tho the margin be formed by a line ever so various; and the extremities ever so artificially concealed. This scene is as grand as any

GILPIN'S DRAWING OF THE TEMPLE OF VENUS

thing within such narrow limits can be. The largeness of the parts gives an idea of vastness much beyond its size. If any thing in it is displeasing, it is the temple, which is in itself no beautiful object, and is besides ill-adapted. If there must be an object, a naid-grotto, quite simple, had been more suitable.

40

*The ground about the temple of Pan is another very beautiful scene. It is a sloping lawn, skirted with wood. At the upper end stands the temple, well adapted to the situation; which is just such a retreat as a shepherd might be supposed to choose for his flock at noon, or evening, affording both pasturage,*

GILPIN'S DRAWING OF THE TEMPLE OF PAN

*and shelter. The building (formed of stumps, and moss, and thatched with chips) is wholly artless, and simple. It is indeed an imitation of Grecian architecture: but Pan himself, it might be supposed, or some of his rustic worshippers might have seen the form, and imitated it with such materials as they found upon the spot. Had it been constructed of hewn stone it had lost its simplicity.*

*The temple of Sylvanus affords another very beautiful scene, still more picturesque than the last. It stands nearly upon the knowl of a woody hill; shaded by trees, and open only in two directions. In front the hill slopes gradually along a lawn, into an open grove; through which it sinks into a dark wood. In the other direction the hill falls precipitately; and through the boles of lofty trees you have a beautiful view of a rich country. Such a foreground gives it the spirit of a landscape. The situation is well adapted to the inhabitant. The place naturally suggests the idea of a wild wood-god, just peeping out to take a distant view of the world, darting instantly into his thicket, if any thing alarm him. This habitation is properly*

41

*furnished with bows and arrows, oaten-pipes, and instruments of husbandry.*

*The Hermitage affords another very beautiful scene, and wholly different from any of the others. It stands upon the steep side of one woody hill, and overlooks another so that the prospect is entirely woody. You look down a precipice, and see nothing but the boles of trees, and brushwood at the bottom: you look across the valley, and take in a short distance; but it is a distance composed only of the foliage of trees seen through the branches of those more at hand. The whole scene is grand, and solemn; the world, and every concern in it, is shut out; and nothing left the hermit, but the heavens to contemplate.*

*From the gloomy scene, you enter into open day, where the last grand prospect breaks in upon you. You see on one side, the smooth declivity of an hill skirted with wood; on the other, a noble tent of hanging woods rising above the trees of the valley.*

*To take a thorough view of all the beauties of the very rich spot, carries you a round of about 5 miles. There are, besides these, very many very beautiful scenes; but these were the most striking.*

*'A spot in the wood, dedicated to the genius of Socrates, seems to me no way adapted.'*


WHILE Gilpin's horse was stabled and fed at Dorking, he made his excursion to the Rookery just beyond Westcott. Much impressed with what he saw, he gives a most valuable account of the estate, the only detailed description we have of Daniel Malthus's residence there. The opening paragraph recording his visit deals with what was to be one of Gilpin's leading topics - the primacy of natural beauty over any contrived improvement of the landscape. Mr Malthouse, 'the late proprietor of the place' found, Gilpin said, the hills a thicket and the water a bed of sedge. 'The woods he has opened in many places; and exhibited a variety of lawns, open groves, and close recesses'. He cleared the water and formed it into a lake. 'Everything is grand, simple and uniform, the purest nature I ever met with in any improvement'.

It was a pity that William Gilpin just missed meeting the 'late proprietor of the place', Daniel Malthus (1730-1800). Now unrecognised except as the father of Thomas, famous for the 'Malthusian' theory of population, he was a man of ideas and, if accounted eccentric, also of great charm.[1] He would certainly have interested his visitor. However, in that very year he had sold the Rookery to Richard Fuller, a London banker, and was, at that moment, if he carried out his earlier plan, with his wife and family in Dijon. He had bought the land in 1759 from Abraham Tucker[2] and in the overgrown woodland and clogged water of the Pippbrook he saw the latent possibilities of 'hill and dale, wood and water' and how he could display them in their 'natural simplicity'. With the rebuilding of the old farmhouse there, he converted the whole into a small but adequate 'gentleman's seat'.[3]

THE ROOKERY IN RICHARD FULLER'S TIME.
THE HOUSE HAS ALREADY BEEN EXTENDED AND CASTELLATED.
ENGRAVED BY J. REDAWAY FROM A DRAWING BY J.P. NEALE

It was this natural simplicity which so pleased Gilpin but, what he experienced directly from the country around him, Daniel Malthus had come to admire partly through precept. Malthus was greatly influenced by Jean-Jacques Rousseau, the champion of 'natural' man as against his 'civilised' counterpart, who advocated the individual development of children in natural surroundings in his book *Emile* and who described an ideal picture of purified characters in a natural garden in his novel *La Nouvelle Héloïse*. Not only did Rousseau captivate Malthus by his ideas but by the magnetism of his personality.[4] They had first met in Switzerland and,

43

ROUSSEAU BOTANISING. EIGHTEENTH CENTURY ENGRAVING BY AN UNKNOWN ARTIST

when Rousseau came to England in 1766-7, Malthus hoped that he would stay at the Rookery and enjoy what he had to show him of his estate and his country home, reminiscent of Emile's. But he was doomed to disappointment; Rousseau's visit was brief; he ignored Malthus' offers of help, boarded in Chiswick and departed unexpectedly to Staffordshire, remaining there to 'botanise' and find peace and quiet. Whether disillusion was a factor in Malthus putting the Rookery up for sale in 1768 we shall never know, but meantime Gilpin saw the grounds as Malthus intended them to be and the house without alteration.

In approving the Rookery as an embodiment of his own ideals, Gilpin set against it 'the greatest profusion of expence' and 'the hand of art' in the layout of Stowe, Painshill and Kew, objecting to polished walks and artificial combinations of planting and the 'forced antithesis' of vistas and objects. The *Stowe Dialogue* of 1748 between Callophilus and Polypthon discussing the layout of the grounds as they walk through Lord Cobham's estate has already been mentioned. Polypthon in the earlier work, apart from a few comments such as the superiority of the prospects in the north of England, waxes enthusiastic about the various walks and vistas and there was no objection to the extravagant scheme of the whole. The reference to Stowe here in 1768 is far more critical. The 'greatest profusion of expence' was certainly evident at Painshill too, which was so richly set out that we can understand how Charles Hamilton, its creator, came to be bankrupted. Gilpin's first visit was in May 1765[5] and, while admiring much, as, for instance, the temple of Bacchus - 'one of the most beautiful things of the kind that I have seen' - he was quite ready to note where he felt that taste had gone astray. Of the grotto, for instance, he writes, '[It] is a whimsical little object . . . It is trifling and unnatural on the spot and at a distance affords no kind of beauty to the whole' - 'whimsical' he uses in the derogatory sense of 'motiveless'. Most of us nowadays are so interested in the restoration of the grotto that we admire rather than criticise. In fact the whole restoration work at Stowe by the National Trust, and that at Cobham by the Painshill Park Trust which gained European recognition in January 1999, seem equally remarkable.

In the same year as his visit to Painshill, Gilpin went to look at Kew which, at that time, bore features comparable to the other two estates though, one would imagine, at a fraction of the cost. He followed the serpentine walk from which one could admire up to twenty buildings, most of which had been constructed by Sir William Chambers. At a distance they looked substantial enough but, as Horace Walpole remarked, they were 'all of wood' except the Pagoda and the Ruined Arch. The Pagoda was flanked by the Alhambra and the Mosque which made, Gilpin thought, a 'disagreeable regularity' - an example of the forced antithesis he found so objectionable. The Pagoda itself he regarded as a 'whimsical object'.[6] At the same time, he drew a delightful sketch from the path with the Theatre of Augusta (his 'Grecian Colonade'), the Temple of Victory in the distance and characteristic trees, though the Palladian Bridge in the foreground he disliked - a 'disagreeable object'.[7]

GILPIN'S DRAWING AT KEW. A VIEW FROM THE SERPENTINE WALK

In these three examples, Gilpin indicated the advantages and the faults in human artistry in relation to natural beauty which similarly preoccupied Daniel Malthus, recalling Rousseau, in setting out the grounds of his country house.

To examine thoroughly 'all the beauties of the very rich spot' that was the Rookery meant a round of about five miles and Gilpin selects what impressed him most. He starts with the lake immediately below the house, but separated from it by a wide lawn and footpath, as shown in John Hassell's later illustration. Here, where Malthus' main task was to clear the waterway, the lake was established to beautiful effect and enhanced by hanging woods. On the small island in the lake, however, among the trees, Malthus had placed his Temple to Venus. It is perhaps worth mentioning that the goddess Venus was celebrated originally as the presider over gardens and her festival was kept as a holiday by gardeners. Gilpin had taken his sketching materials and her 'ill-adapted' classical building is indicated with pencil and grey wash and suggests something too large and bare for its position. The 'naiad grotto', which he would prefer, had currency all over Europe, the simplest type being a recessed fountain where often the statue of a sleeping nymph or water-spirit invited quiet contemplation. Later he was to admire an example at Stourhead, quoting its inscription, translated from the Latin by Alexander Pope:

> Nymph of the grot these sacred springs I keep
> And to the murmur of these waters sleep
> Ah spare my slumbers gently tread the cave
> And drink in silence or in silence lave[8]

Gilpin remained wary, as seen throughout his writings, of marring picturesque scenes by adding showy ornamental buildings - 'all the laboured works of art' such as temples, obelisks and Chinese bridges that suggested inharmonious ideas, as he wrote in *Forest Scenery*.[9] However, at the Rookery the classically simple but rustic Temple to Pan,[10] the half-goatish guardian of the flocks, fitted its setting most successfully as did the Temple of

TEMPLE TO PAN FROM JOHN TIMBS, *A PICTURESQUE PROMENADE ROUND DORKING* (2ND EDITION, 1823)

Sylvanus, the woodland god. He loved, too, the varied surfaces of the scene 'where the ground swells and falls' with hanging lawns, screened with woods, connecting the valleys. The Hermitage, also, was so placed that both the foreground and the distance mirrored trees and fine foliage; the world was shut out and the hermit had just 'the heavens to contemplate'.

Usually, as at Painshill and at many other places, not forgetting Queen Caroline's at Kew, hermitages (and their hermits) provided a diversion for the visitor. For Gilpin, the harmony of nature and art was paramount. This was why he felt the spot dedicated to Socrates 'in no way adapted' - unable to call up the great and wise philosopher naturally - but here he breaks off without any further detail.

THE ROOKERY, ENGRAVED BY T. BARBER FROM A DRAWING BY H. GASTINEAU (1819)

There Gilpin left the Rookery, conscious of the 'very many very beautiful scenes' which he had to abandon through lack of time. It is interesting to note that many years after Malthus had left Westcott, he would seem to have allied himself with Gilpin's views on the picturesque when he told Humphry Repton how important he felt 'painting principles' were in any improvement of land[11] - finally severing himself from his erstwhile master, Rousseau.

The Rookery after Malthus left remained in the hands of the Fullers until 1892, the house being much extended and castellated, losing the simplicity of Emile's 'petite maison de campagne'. Nevertheless, over half a century later, John Timbs described the estate as 'this enchanting spot, unparalleled in rusticity and picturesque effect'. The Temple to Pan was still in place, the pediment 'resembling tree trunks', the sides filled with laths and moss and the front closed off by a fence formed of 'limbs of trees', and could have been little changed. It had an inscription '*Pan curat oves ovumque magistros*' (Pan guardian of sheep and their shepherds) - possibly added later as Gilpin did not mention it - however, the back proved to be utilised as a cow-house. Timbs speaks lyrically of the glassy lake and bubbling streams, of the variety of trees and shrubs on the island and of the borders of the water with 'their craggy precipices and retired glens . . . abounding with delightful nooks'.[12]

By 1849, the Rookery as described by W. J. Keane is evidently still most beautiful. He praises the beech woods and the groves of oak and the yews, particularly noticeable as he approaches from the Tillingbourne to the lakes with their clear water, the further joined to the one by the house by a waterfall. As he neared the house with its planting, he felt that the scene 'was moulded by nature and embellished by art'. By then, with its flower gardens, the pleasure-grounds, conservatories and ample kitchen gardens, it was much more in line with the other Surrey gentlemen's residences, except for the sheer size of land and other property that the Fullers had acquired over the years. Six hundred and fifty acres in all went for auction

THE ROOKERY. VIEW OF THE ESTATE FROM THE 1894 SALE PARTICULARS

in 1894, broken into lots after George Fuller's death. No longer were the carts bearing the Fuller name from his various farms to be seen in the vicinity. The greatest days of the Rookery were over though it was still an elegant estate until the middle of World War II, the house itself unchanged, its frontage covered with wisteria, magnolia and clematis and the lawns in front protected from the footpath by a fine hedge. Mr Brooke of Brooke Bond's tea was the last private owner.

When, in 1942, it was bought by Universal Estates for 'development', they undertook to 'keep the beauties of the Rookery estate, admired by thousands of hikers', intact, as the *Dorking Advertiser* put it.[13] In the event, the house was converted into ten flats, a move which was not a great success. By 1964, its parapets and pinnacles crowned a ruined shell surrounded by rubble and weed and it was demolished four years later. In its place has arisen an incongruous row of ten 'town houses'. The footpath still runs between them and the lake, which is almost hidden by a tangle of saplings and undergrowth, though there are much older trees among them. The whole is protected by barbed wire.

If it is hard to re-create what Malthus achieved and William Gilpin so much admired, there are two happy reminiscences in the fact that a copse beyond the Rookery is still called Sylvanus Wood and one of the fields is named Pan Meadow.[14]

MORRIS CHARMAN, WHO WORKED FOR GEORGE FULLER, DRIVING ONE OF THE FARM CARTS. THE NAME FULLER IS JUST DISCERNIBLE. THE PHOTOGRAPH DATES FROM SOME TIME BEFORE 1880

NOTES TO CHAPTER IV

1 His son and relatives recognised Malthus's attractive personality but his granddaughter Louisa Bray recorded a different view: 'My grandfather's character was peculiar and his opinions on some subjects eccentric'. Recollections (1857), Surrey History Centre, G85/23/1.
2 See previous chapter, note 3.
3 Rev. O. Manning and W. Bray, *The History and Antiquities of the County of Surrey* (1804-12, 4 vols.), vol. 1, p. 259. It was Malthus who renamed the estate the Rookery.
4 Jean Jacques Rousseau's extraordinary personality and Malthus's devotion to him and his ideas are vividly shown in the relevant letters in R.A. Leigh, *Correspondance Complète de Rousseau* (1977). It is meticulously indexed and the French used by the eighteenth century English easy to follow! All background references here are taken from the letters. See also Maurice Cranston, *The Solitary Self*, vol. 3 of his biography of Rousseau, (1997).
5 Bodleian Library, MS.Eng. misc. e 522. The full text, his sketchbook of Painshill and his subsequent visit is now published with commentary by Michael Symes (Barn Elms, 1994).
6 Ibid. (bound with the notebook as above).
7 Ibid.
8 Alexander Pope, *Minor Poems* (Norman Ault and John Butt (eds.), 1954), p. 248. This edition gives the history of the inscription and the original Latin text, 'that beautiful antique one which you know I am so fond of', as Pope wrote in 1725.
9 Vol. 1, section 2 on Parks.
10 Again sketched quickly as for the Temple of Venus.
11 Referred to by David Jacques, *Georgian Gardens* (1990 paperback), pp. 151-2.
12 *A Picturesque Promenade round Dorking* (1823), p. 123.
13 Details and many photographs of the later history of the Rookery are held in the archive of the Dorking Museum.
14 The name 'Pan Meadow' appears in the auction details of 1894 when the estate was split up. (Information kindly provided by David Webb of the Westcott Local History Group).

EXTRACT FROM JOHN ROCQUE, *MAP OF SURREY*, SURVEYED *C.* 1760. BY 1766 THE MANOR OF NORBURY
WAS IN THE HANDS OF ANTHONY CHAPMAN. IT HAD BEEN IN CHARLES TRYON'S FAMILY SINCE 1731

# CHAPTER V - DORKING TO LEATHERHEAD

*'Near Dorking, at Dibden, Mr Howard, heir to the D. of Norfolk, is building a very handsome house. It stands high; is skreened by a wood behind it, and commands a noble view of the vale of the Mole, of which the boundary is Boxhill, which seen in perspective is a fine object. The other parts of the view are not very picturesque.*

*From Dorking to Mickleham, and from thence to Leatherhead, is the sweetest ride imaginable. Box-hill is a grand object on the right, which accompanies you great part of the way. In itself it is [a] large, mishapen mass - vast, unbroken denseness(?) with little variety. The first part of it is covered with box; it then shows the chalk in large shelving currents from its sides(?), the box struggling with the chalk: the third part of it is a downy declivity. The line at the top in every part almost unbroken; and has as little variety as so long a line almost can have. The Mole runs at the bottom of it, but is hid from the eye by the hedges of the lane. The large trees which grow upon the banks of the river are of great service in giving space and distance to the hill. It is seen best just at the end of Dorking where it appears in proper perspective. On the left Lady Trion's park\* affords a beautiful view. It is a rising lawn of firm turf ornamented with clumps. On the right, we passed by a low thatched cottage, lately belonging to Mr Re . . . , on which a great deal of money has been thrown away. It is full of littlenesses and trifling objects. It might be made a pretty place if every thing was undone which has been done.*

*From Mickleham the high grounds on the right, and the meadows on the left, through which the Mole flows, whose course is marked by lofty alders make a pleasing contrast.'*

---

\*Because of the importance of 'Lady Trion's park' (i.e. Norbury), both to Gilpin in the 1770s and for its interest since, the commentary on Norbury follows separately at the end of the comments on the Mole Valley.

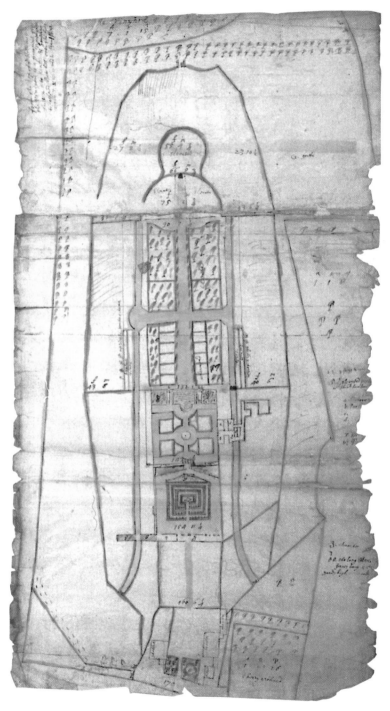

JOHN AUBREY'S SKETCH PLAN OF THE HON. CHARLES HOWARD'S GARDEN
IN THE DEEPDENE, *C.* 1673. THE VINEYARD IS AT THE TOP OF THE PLAN
WITH THE ORCHARDS AND FORMAL GARDENS BELOW

O N his way home from the Rookery Gilpin would have left the
Deepdene (Dibden) to the south-east where, on the rising ground to
the side of the dene, the new house was sited. The Hon. Charles Howard,
who inherited the property as a child, was then of an age to decide to make
the hundred acre estate his country home. A painting of about 1780[1] shows
the house standing high as Gilpin says, 'skreened by a wood behind it', with
the stables to the left at the base of the dene and a temple crowning the
rising ground. The Deepdene had already enjoyed an interesting history
under the Hon. Charles' grandfather, Charles Howard of Greystoke,[2] who
lived there from 1652 until his death in 1713. Of his 'cottage of retirement
where he withdrew from the wicked world'[3] there is no trace, but he is
known for his scientific studies, building himself a laboratory for his
experiments and contributing papers to the Royal Society.[4] Among other
activities, he made a remarkable collection of flowers and grasses of the
Surrey countryside, all carefully pressed, mounted and labelled in a thick
book; five varieties on one page, for example, of hellebore, another of
mints - between two and three hundred in all. The pages are bound
between heavy boards covered with leather, the front embossed with his
name, date (1660) and place, Darking (Dorking). The volume measures
about 45 x 27 x 16 centimetres and, after nearly 250 years, is in frail
condition, though the green of the leaves of specimens is still intense and

JAMES CANTER, *THE DEEPDENE, SURREY, SEEN IN A PROSPECT OVER DORKING* (*C.* 1773 OR 1783)

some colour remains in the flowers. With John Aubrey's help we can visualise the actual garden;[5] he drew a plan of it and wrote a description of the formal beds and paths, the walks 'bordured with thyme' along the sides of the 'amphitheatre' (dene), the rare plants, the orchards and the high south terrace with its tunnel below and the vineyard on its southern slopes,[6] which Defoe said 'has produced since most excellent good wine'.[7]

Like his grandfather, Gilpin's Charles Howard was a scholar and a writer, belonging to the Royal Society and the Society of Antiquaries. He remodelled the garden, relaxing the original formal setting and his wife, too, was interested - she had a hermitage built there 'with all the requisites for a holy anchorite [hermit]'.[8] Charles succeeded as tenth Duke of Norfolk in 1777, but continued to spend his summers at the Deepdene. He died in 1786. Their son, the eleventh Duke, was more concerned with the repair of Arundel Castle and, four years after he inherited the property, he sold it to Sir William Burrell, Commissioner of Excise. In poor health, Sir William died in 1796 and his son in due course auctioned the estate, described in the sale catalogue of 1807 as having among other features, a 'beautifully diversified pleasure ground, planted with luxurious forest trees ... tastefully arranged with walks, rural retirements, grottos, caverns, and a terrace' with extensive views over 'enchanting country'.

Under its new owners, the Hopes,[9] the estate entered its grandest phase, sustained until 1912. An art connoisseur, designer and collector, patron of painters and sculptors, Thomas Hope chose the Deepdene for his country residence, adding considerably to the estate between 1818 and 1823, making major alterations and additions to the house. David Watkin, in his *Thomas Hope, 1769-1831, and the Neo-classical Idea* (1964), gives a vivid impression of

Height 11¼ Inches.

the transformation that took place. The mansion with its highly decorated, irregular terraces with small flights of steps, its parterres with massed flowers, became an early model for the fashionable Italianate style. One of the additions was a south-west wing which included a new sculpture gallery, conservatories and orangeries. Mr & Mrs Hope's many guests, among them such personages as Walter Scott and Humphry Davy, recorded their tributes in the Deepdene album.

Thomas Hope held the position of Sheriff of Surrey in 1828 and died highly respected in 1831. He was succeeded by Henry Thomas Hope, his eldest son, who acquired more land including Betchworth, as already mentioned, bringing the estate to about twelve miles in circumference. He shared his father's interest in architecture and made further extensive changes to the house, including remodelling both the entrance and garden fronts. He entered politics and became a supporter of Disraeli and his Young England movement, with meetings often held at the Deepdene. Disraeli dedicated to Thomas Hope his novel *Coningsby* (1884), the first of a trilogy and the first truly political novel in England, 'conceived and partly executed among the glades and galleries of the Deepdene'.

The Deepdene was scarred by the railway twice; it cut through the estate in 1849 and again in 1867, five years after Henry Hope's death. His wife continued to live in the mansion until her death in 1884. It was then that its fortunes began to falter. Mrs Hope bequeathed the freehold estates to her second grandson, Lord Francis Hope. Without settling at the Deepdene, he used the estate chiefly for shooting parties, but ran into serious debt and was declared bankrupt in 1894. The Deepdene was leased

Height 2 Feet 7 Inches.

VASES FROM THE COLLECTION OF
THOMAS HOPE, ENGRAVED
BY HENRY MOSES

57

to the Dowager Duchess of Marlborough who maintained it in appropriate manner and, with her third husband, Sir William Beresford, entertained friends freely with the shooting, with balls and other evening events, and fulfilled the role of Lady of the Manor for Dorking with generosity and kindliness. The estate, with its beautiful trees, azaleas and exotics, prospered.

*DEEPDENE, THE SEAT OF THOMAS HOPE, ESQ.,*
WATERCOLOUR ON PENCIL BY JOHN HASSELL (1823)

The Duchess died in 1909 and from then on the Deepdene's fortunes little by little declined. Lord Francis' property was in the hands of the receivers by 1912 and the mansion went through various changes, the major part of the contents sold by Christies in 1917 and the building becoming a residential hotel from 1920. The estate was gradually broken up and sold for housing development and, in the 1930s, the Dorking by-pass cut through the grounds of the hotel which was by then failing. On the outbreak of World War II, it was bought as an emergency measure by the Southern Railway and the interior treated with little respect. In a deplorable state, it was finally demolished in 1967 and replaced with modern offices. Kuoni Travel bought both the building and the immediate grounds in 1990. A little of the estate is still in public hands; part of the dene (very overgrown) and, importantly, the old terrace area and its avenue and approach and a little surrounding land. The Dorking and District Preservation Society, with the support of Ralph Vaughan Williams, was effectively involved in what was saved and is still actively engaged in trying to provide clearance and access.[10]

William Gilpin would deplore the present unfortunate state of affairs and, as for the office block, he would certainly find it 'ill-adapted' - and as far from the 'natural' taste he always sought as it is possible to imagine.

WATERCOLOUR OF THE DEEPDENE BY WILLIAM BARTLETT (1825)
SHOWING THE DENE FROM THE TERRACE

GILPIN mounted his horse again at Dorking and turned north along the old road to Mickleham; 'from thence to Leatherhead is the sweetest ride imaginable'. When so much has changed, new roads built, old houses vanished under increasing modern development, it is Box Hill[11] and its river, the Mole, that links us most directly with William Gilpin's journey on that August day. What impressed him most about the hill was its vastness - a 'large mishapen mass . . . with little variety', its chalkiness startling then as now, the woods, chiefly of box, with isolated box trees managing to grow virtually on the chalk and then the open downland itself. Today, although the box has declined in quantity, the actual woodland has increased, with yew, oak and beech particularly noticeable, the latter on the high ground slowly recovering from the devastating storms of 1987 and 1990.

*VIEW FROM BOX HILL, LOOKING TOWARDS NORBURY PARK (C. 1840).*
A VICTORIAN GROUP ENJOYING A DAY OUT

Approaching Box Hill as he did from Dorking, Gilpin with his eye for pictorial qualities noticed how the large trees on the banks of the Mole gave 'space and distance' to the scene; this apart, he saw the hill as noble rather than picturesque, lacking, as he thought, enough variety of line for his taste. It was not until some years later, when he studied it from the vantage point of Norbury Park, that he revised his opinion. From there it made 'a side screen' to the picture across the valley, 'filling its station with great beauty, discovering its shivering precipices and downy hillocks, everywhere interspersed with the mellow verdure of box tinged with red and orange'.[12]

The box, which Gilpin much admired, is of very ancient origin and has been prized for centuries for use and, since the seventeenth century, also for enjoyment. John Evelyn in his diary of 1655[13] describes his visit to see 'those rare natural bowers, cabinets and shady walks in the box coppses and the goodly walks around' and Daniel Defoe in the 1720s wrote of the ladies and gentlemen from Epsom coming to walk in the boxwoods on Sundays, their behaviour causing considerable gossip locally.[14] By the early 1800s Box Hill was known as the 'Cockneys' Paradise'[15] from the number of Londoners who visited there in the summer. T. A. Yeates was only one of many who expressed their delight at the views from the top. 'I was yesterday afternoon', he writes, 'surveying with inexpressible pleasure

*BUXUS SEMPERVIRENS*
(COMMON BOX)

the almost unparalleled beauties of the surrounding scene, while sitting on a verdant sod . . .'[16] Subsequently, of course, with the advent of the railway, the influx of visitors - day trippers - increased enormously and today the area draws over a million people a year. Most of Box Hill is now owned by the National Trust and is a designated country park; at 634 feet, it exhibits 'a great variety of pleasing views' as Gilpin truly said. Indeed they are unsurpassed and, from the Salomons' memorial,[17] Chanctonbury Ring and the Devil's Dyke can be easily picked out.

Box Hill forms the corner of the gap through which the Mole runs, as have all communications since the Roman Stane Street linked Chichester with London. The Mole is described by Gilpin as a lazy stream which is a true description of its flow, the drop in contour being small. It had long been recognised as such; John Milton[18] and Alexander Pope[19] both referring to it as 'sullen', while, later, verses attributed to Mrs Barbauld

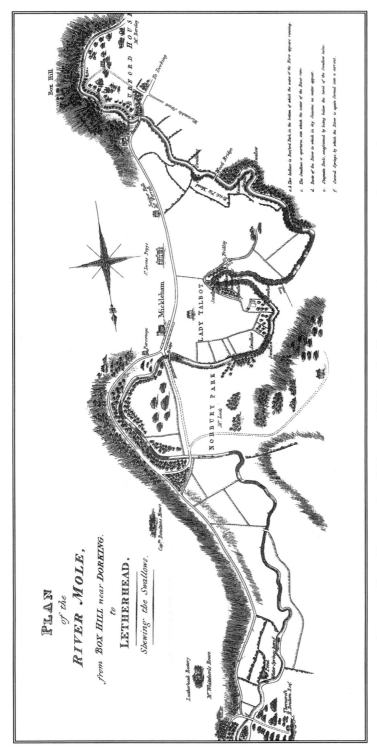

MAP OF THE RIVER MOLE FROM REV. O. MANNING & W. BRAY, *THE HISTORY AND ANTIQUITIES OF THE COUNTY OF SURREY*

(1743-1824), a writer and popular poet, speak of Box Hill and the Mole in these terms:

> From the smoke and the din and the hurry of town
> Let the care-wearied cit[**] to this spot hasten down . . .
>
> . . . Here may Industry, Peace and Contentment reign still
> While the Mole softly creeps at the foot of the hill.

The name of the river has been discussed for very many years;[20] whether it is a formation from Molesey where it runs into the Thames, which is more probable, or is taken from its habit of burrowing underground through its famous 'swallow-holes', found only between the Burford and Leatherhead bridges, is still debated. William Gilpin noted that it sank 'under the ground in some places' and by these channels or 'swallows' the river bed is left almost dry in parts in hot weather. His praise for the Mole is moderate. He notes its beauty in various parts, especially where it runs below Norbury Park with its banks fringed with alders and 'Mr Lock's woods and trees rise loftily above'.[21]    William Gilpin commented on two further features as he passed through Mickleham: the first, a beautiful park,

BURFORD BRIDGE AND BOX HILL.
ENGRAVED BY W. WALLIS FROM A DRAWING BY H. GASTINEAU (1819)

---

**citizen; Cockney

and the other, 'a low thatched cottage'.[22] Of the latter, he certainly does not spare criticism; on it, he says, a great deal of money has been wasted. Which cottage and who had lived there it is impossible now to say for certain. The owner's name is not verifiable from Gilpin's manuscript as, after the first few letters, 'Mr Re . . .', the rest is hidden by the binding and, even if it were not, there seem to be no records of the time to make any sure identification. His remarks on the 'littlenesses and trifling objects' there, however, suggest that the cottage had been intended for a country retreat or 'cottage orné' and embellished quite inappropriately.

Mickleham, like other areas of Surrey convenient for London, saw, in the eighteenth century, the gradual gentrification of its farmland and, moreover, the acquisition of cottages by the leisured classes. An interesting account in the *Gentleman's Magazine* of 1787[23] describes a visit to Mickleham, 'a place deservedly a favourite in which several cottages have been filled up in a very neat manner and have been inhabited by persons of fashion'. The writer goes on to mention 'a small thatched cottage [that] was built by Mr Ryves (Reeves?) about thirty years ago' - about the right date - in a gravel pit adjoining the road, which it is very tempting to identify with the 'low thatched' building that Gilpin so roundly criticised.

In Gilpin's *Western Tour* he points out how difficult it is for a 'gentleman' to preserve the proper nature of a cottage. There should be no stonework, such as architrave or frieze, or ornament of any kind. If, for example, a porch were to be added, it should be of 'common brick' with a plain neat roof. No splendour inside, though of course, alterations for the ordinary conveniences of living would be permissible. Typically he adds that one must never aim for artificial elegance but at 'the pure simplicities of nature'.[24]

However, by far the more significant of Gilpin's two observations was that concerning the adjacent beautiful park, that of Norbury. As yet unknown to him, the next owner was to become his esteemed and, in many ways, close friend, notable on his own account and of lasting importance in the annals of Surrey.

NOTES TO CHAPTER V

1   The painting, often reproduced, is attributed to James Canter. It hangs at Lords Cricket Ground, home of the MCC. Canter (*c.* 1771-83), a topographical artist, painted views of the estates of several Roman Catholic peers; three of Arundel Castle are still in the Duke's possession.
2   As attested by the Howard Genealogical Tables; Arundel Castle archives.
3   Aubrey's *Antiquities*, vol. 3, p. 211.

4   H. K. S. Causton, *The Howard Papers* (1862)

5   Bodleian Library, Eng.MS.Aubrey 4, ff.49-50; see also explanatory drawing repro-
    duced from it in D. Mercer and A. Jackson, *The Deepdene Dorking* (Dorking and District
    Preservation Society, revised edition 1996).

6   Aubrey's *Antiquities*, vol. 4, pp. 164-7.

7   Daniel Defoe, *A Tour through the Whole Island of Great Britain* (1724), Letter 2, p. 162,
    (ed. Pat Rogers, Penguin repd. 1986).

8   John Timbs, *A Picturesque Promenade round Dorking* (1823), p. 267.

9   This account of the Hopes' important tenure of the Deepdene is based on two
    excellent sources: David Watkin's, as mentioned in the text, and Doris Mercer's and
    Alan Jackson's (see above). Detailed references are therefore not provided.

10  In 1996, the Society commissioned a valuable survey of the area from Cazenove
    Architects' Cooperative which includes a preliminary archaeological survey by the
    RCHME, giving a needed basis for progress towards public enjoyment of what
    remains to us of the Deepdene.

11  A very good survey of Box Hill is available from the National Trust together with a
    number of striking photographs: *Box Hill, Surrey* (1997).

12  *Western Tour* (1798).

13  E. S. de Beer (ed.), John Evelyn's *Diary* - 27 August 1655.

14  *A Tour through the Whole Island . . .*, (see above, note 7), p. 163.

15  W. Thorne, *The Garden of Surrey* (Langley, Dorking, 1829), p. 32.

16  See the *Monthly Magazine* (November 1815), p. 321.

17  Leopold Salomons, the then owner of Norbury Park, bought the 230 acres of Box Hill
    which came on the open market in 1912 and in 1914 most generously presented the
    area to the National Trust.

18  *At a Vacation Exercise* (1627).

19  *Windsor Forest* (1711).

20  See the Leatherhead and District Local History Society, *Proceedings*, vol. 5, no. 2 (1998-9).

21  There is an opportunity to see the Mole's 'swallows', and to assess its attractions, more
    easily now that the local councils and other local bodies are providing a trail running
    from Leatherhead Bridge along the river and then on to Dorking and Westhumble.

22  'Cottage' was an elastic term at the time. Jane Austen in *Sense and Sensibility* (first
    published in 1811 but begun in the mid-1790s) describes the cottage to which the
    Dashwoods moved as small and compact, but it had two sitting-rooms, four bedrooms
    and two garrets. It was not, however, a 'cottage orné'. With her fine irony, she writes,
    'as a cottage it was defective, for the building was regular, the roof was tiled, the
    window shutters were not painted green, nor were the walls covered with honeysuckle'
    (chap. 6).

23  The *Gentleman's Magazine Library* (1900), part 2, pp. 963-5.

24  *Western Tour*, section 35, p. 308.

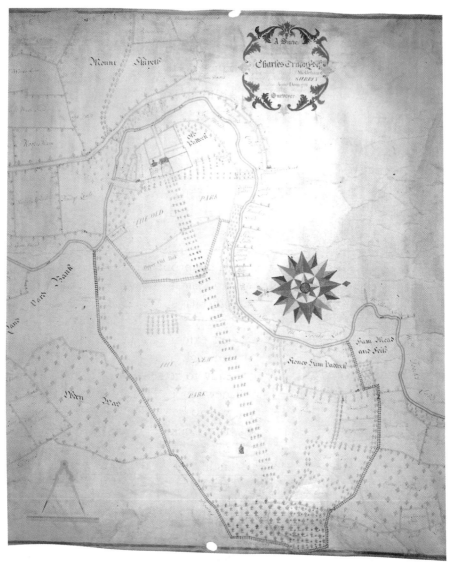

A SECTION OF AN ESTATE MAP OF NORBURY
DRAWN BY TYCHO WING FOR CHARLES TRYON IN 1731.

THE MAP ILLUSTRATES AN OPEN LANDSCAPE WITH THREE FORMAL AVENUES RADIATING FROM THE MANOR HOUSE LOCATED ON LOW LYING LAND, CLOSE TO THE RIVER MOLE. ONE AVENUE APPEARS TO CUT ACROSS THE CONTOURS OF THE DOWNLAND SLOPE, TERMINATING AT A HIGH POINT ADJACENT TO WHAT IS NOW CALLED DRUIDS GROVE (AN AREA OF SUBSTANTIAL YEW TREES ON THE SLOPE OVERLOOKING THE MOLE GAP). THE PARK IS DIVIDED INTO THREE UNITS, THE OLD PARK, UPPER OLD PARK AND THE NEW PARK; THE NEW PARK PALE IS SHOWN AS TREE LINED WHILST THE OLD PARK AND UPPER OLD PARK APPEAR TO BE SEPARATED BY A FIELD BOUNDARY, DEPICTED WITH OCCASIONAL TREES. A 'SUMMER HOUSE' IS SHOWN IN NEW PARK ADJACENT TO THE LONG AVENUE. SOME PERIPHERAL AREAS ARE REPRESENTED AS WOODED (AN AREA OF 'COPPICE' FOR INSTANCE, AT THE WESTERN END OF NEW PARK) AND TWO AREAS OF PLANTATION OR WOODLAND ARE ALSO LOCATED ON THE CREST OF THE DOWNS. THE OVERALL IMPRESSION, HOWEVER, IS OF AN OPEN LANDSCAPE.[1]

66

# CHAPTER VI
## NORBURY PARK AND WILLIAM LOCK

WILLIAM LOCK FROM A PORTRAIT BY
THOMAS LAWRENCE

THE park with its 'rising lawn' was part of the Manor of Norbury inherited by Colonel Tryon. The manor house with its tree-lined avenue and formal gardens was situated on the bend of the River Mole at the north of Mickleham and his wife, Lady Mary, continued to live there after the Colonel's death. By 1766, however, her son, who had inherited the property, sold it on to Anthony Chapman. Said to be a land speculator who apparently made a considerable profit from selling many of the valuable walnut trees cultivated extensively in the manorial area, Chapman neglected the manor house and was quite ready to re-sell the estate in 1774.[2] It was its new owner, William Lock, with whom Gilpin was to be closely associated.

William Lock, a connoisseur of the fine arts and a man of means,[3] had spent some years in Italy with his young wife, Frederica Schaub, and had already formed an art collection in Rome before he returned to England and settled at Norbury. While a new house, designed by Thomas Sandby, was being completed on the ridge of the downland, the Locks lived at the run-down manor house as marked on the 1775 edition of Rocque's map. Through mutual acquaintances, William Gilpin and William Lock met and formed a lasting friendship on the basis of their shared interest in art and love of landscape. 'I really think you have more picturesque

FREDERICA LOCK, BY DOWMAN

erudition than any man I know', wrote Gilpin to his friend in 1782,[4] and Norbury Park in Lock's time became a fine example of the picturesque.

Gilpin gives an account of Norbury's main features at the beginning of his 'Observations' made on his *Western Tour* of 1775, which he added to and published in 1798. Its beautiful views reached to the South Downs, a little marred perhaps by several other proprietors' houses in the distance, but the nearer scenes were unreservedly pleasing. He describes the woodland walk on the 'downy hill' to the right of the south front of the house, winding along the slope and giving glimpses of the valley below, some of them 'seen through the spreading arms of an oak or beech' acting as a frame of a picture. The other

SCENE IN NORBURY PARK, *c.* 1780.
WATERCOLOUR BY GEORGE BARRETT, PAINTER OF THE LANDSCAPES IN NORBURY'S DRAWING-ROOM

side-screen of the valley was the 'celebrated Box Hill' contributing its beauties - as referred to earlier. The descent from the north side was even more picturesque with its 'oblique sweeps of descending foregrounds' making the whole what he imagined as being 'a good Alpine picture'.

The house itself, Gilpin thought, was unpretentious but contained a remarkable drawing-room which was soon to become famous for the painted landscapes on three of its walls, cleverly uniting with the loveliness of the natural scene outside. They were executed by George Barrett (1728-84), well known for his landscape canvases, with the help of Gilpin's

A PHOTOGRAPH OF THE DRAWING-ROOM AT NORBURY HOUSE
SHOWING THE PAINTED WALLS AS PRESERVED IN LEOPOLD SALOMON'S TIME.
THE CEILING WAS ALSO PAINTED WITH TRELLIS DECORATION BY PASTORINI

brother Sawrey for the animals and Giovanni Cipriani (1727-1785) for the figures. The west wall was 'taken from the lakes of Cumberland . . . a large portion of the lake under a splendid calm is spread before the eye . . . The near ground is composed of bold rocks and other rough surfaces with which the banks of lakes commonly abound. Among these a wild torrent variously broken pours its water under the surbase of the room, which intercepts it. This torrent,' writes Gilpin, 'the painter has managed so well that its spirit and brilliancy produce no lights which interfere with the calm resplendency of the lake but rather contrast it.'

Gilpin had criticised the torrent earlier[5] as drawing too much attention to itself and interfering with the harmony of the whole, a harmony indispensable both in art and in nature, as he had already noted in his comments on the Rookery. The eastern and northern walls are also described with admiration - 'sylvan' pictures in keeping with the west wall. All corners of the room were decorated with trellis-work, climbing plants and flowers to give the spectators the impression of looking out from an arbour. Finally, Gilpin noted that, at certain times, the pictured light coincided with the setting sun through the windows so that 'all the landscape within and without the room appears illumined by the same sun'.

A lively exchange of views continued between Lock and Gilpin, partly on occasional visits but chiefly by correspondence, for William Gilpin had moved to Boldre in 1777. Most topics concerned aesthetic matters but Lock also sought his friend's views on other subjects, especially about his oldest boy's behaviour. Gilpin on his part dedicated his late publication *Three Essays* to him. Norbury society continued to flourish and included art lovers and artists[6] such as Sir Thomas Lawrence, Henry Fuseli and Turner. But even more lasting fame was to come to this part of Surrey from other sources.

*Norbury Park seen from meadows on the road from Leatherhead* [ to Dorking].
Watercolour on pencil by John Hassell (1822)

FANNY BURNEY READING, FROM A PENCIL
DRAWING BY HER COUSIN EDWARD BURNEY

In April 1784, when in London, William and Frederica Lock had met Frances (Fanny) Burney who had swept into public notice with her novel *Evelina* (1778) and then, with another equally popular, *Cecilia* (1782). Their acquaintance blossomed. 'She [Mrs Lock] does truly interest both head and heart. I love her already',[7] wrote Fanny in her journal which she kept for her favourite sister Susan, wife of an attractive but irresponsible naval officer, Captain Phillips. In July, Fanny made her first visit to Norbury Park. She quickly responded to the happiness of the Lock household and its intellectual stimulus. There in October she wrote that William Lock was 'all instruction, information and intelligence, his invariable sweetness as well as judgment' leaving nothing to be desired.[8]

In the Park itself she loved the wooded walks with their vistas, as Gilpin had, noting the variety of the ground and the striking form of the hills with their changing gleams of wintry light when she visited again in November. Nevertheless, she wrote, were she in a desert, company such as the Locks would make it gay and cheery.[9] In between visits, Frederica maintained a lively correspondence as she scribbled away 'in the fern house' and, on more than one occasion, sending off flowers from her prized gardens. 'Did not my Fanny like the sight when she opened up the box of all those smiling roses?' she wrote in 1789 when Fanny by then was miserably serving out her stint as Second Keeper of the Robes with the Royal Family.

71

The Queen she much admired but the strict court etiquette she found totally exhausting. Of the little time she had to herself, she managed an hour at breakfast. On one such occasion she records, 'I have a book for my companion... My present book is Gilpin's description of the Lakes of Cumberland and Westmoreland. Mrs Delany has lent it me. It is the most picturesque reading I ever met with; it shows me landscapes of every sort ... I forget I am but reading and fancy I see them before me, coloured by the hand of nature.'[10]

The link between the Locks and the Burneys was further strengthened when Susan and her husband came to live in Mickleham in 1785. They rented a cottage, now demolished, opposite the 'Old House' and Susan, in particular, as her husband was often absent, became intimate with the hospitable William and Frederica Lock. However, in 1792, further newcomers to Mickleham were to add to the district's notability. Their arrival is attested to by a plaque at the entrance to what is now the well-established Field Studies Centre, Juniper Hall. It reads, 'This house gave shelter in 1792 to a group of progressive French aristocrats who fled to England to escape the worst excesses of the French Revolution ...' They escaped with few possessions and little money. Susan Phillips, living so near and a fluent French speaker,[11] together with the Locks, as best they could

JUNIPER HALL AROUND 1800 FROM A WATERCOLOUR, DATE AND ARTIST UNKNOWN.
THE FIGURE WITH THE STICK IS THOUGHT TO BE TALLEYRAND

72

THE PLAQUE OUTSIDE JUNIPER HALL

The plaque text reads:

- JUNIPER HALL -

This house gave shelter in 1792 to a group of progressive French aristocrats who had fled to England to escape the worst excesses of the French Revolution.
The group included the Princesse de Hénin, the Comtesse de la Châtre, Madame de Staël, Jaucourt, Louis de Narbonne, Lally Tollendal, Alexandre d'Arblay and Talleyrand.
It was here that Fanny Burney the novelist, as a visitor to her sister, Susanna Phillips of Mickleham, met Alexandre d'Arblay to whom she was subsequently married at Mickleham Church.

Given by European School - Brussels I. 1994

helped the group, among whose first arrivals were the Comte de Narbonne, Madame de Staël and Narbonne's friend, General Alexandre d'Arblay. D'Arblay, courageous, open and unaffected in manner, cultured, made a very favourable impression on Susan and when early in 1793 he and Fanny met they felt an immediate affinity. The story of their subsequent courtship and its 'happy ever after ending' is as romantic a one as can be found in any of Fanny's own novels. Braving her otherwise much revered father whose displeasure was based mainly on d'Arblay's lack of means and prospects, Fanny at forty and Alexandre a little younger, were, with the full approval of the Locks, married at Mickleham church the following July. There is an account at the west end of the church to commemorate the day. The outwardly confor- mist, retiring figure that was Fanny Burney hid a talented and deep-feeling person whose action succeeded in astoni- shing most of her friends.

Dr Burney was reconciled in due course and the d'Arblays continued to live in the area; first, briefly, at Phoenice Farm (since re-built) near Polesden Lacey, 'in a most beautiful and healthful situation', then, until 1797, renting a cottage at Great Bookham[12] where their first and only child, Alexander, was born. This, the Hermitage, so

MONSIEUR D'ARBLAY, C. 1793

73

THE HERMITAGE AT GREAT BOOKHAM
AS IT IS TODAY WITH ADDITIONS

named by Fanny, is almost opposite the church. The extensions, east and west, blend in well with the original dwelling and it is easy to imagine the life there; Fanny, new to house-keeping, seeking recipes from her family and the General developing a great interest in the garden, growing vegetables with enthusiasm if rather limited knowledge, 'pruning' the fruit trees to the consternation of the landlady and cutting the hedge or rather 'mowing it down', as Fanny describes it, with his sabre. Meanwhile, William Lock had offered them a building plot and the d'Arblays gratefully accepted the gift of a five acre field at Westhumble. Fanny determined to compose a new novel which she hoped would pay for a small house designed by her husband, to be built there. The novel, *Camilla*, was finished by 1796 and bought eagerly by her hundreds of admirers. It was financially a complete success but it did not match her earlier achievement and today seems only just readable. However, Camilla Cottage was built, with rising prices, at a cost of over £1,300, this despite

CAMILLA COTTAGE. WATERCOLOUR

74

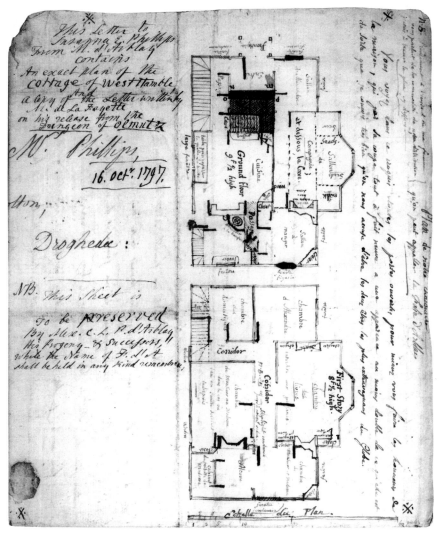

PLANS FOR CAMILLA COTTAGE DRAWN BY MONSIEUR D'ARBLAY

Alexandre helping out with sections of the work himself. By October 1797, the d'Arblays were established in their own home, happy despite their continuing concern about the events in France. Pride of place was given to 'our dearest Mr Lock, our founder's portrait' and among their first visitors were the Princesse de Hénin and M. Lally-Tollendal from Juniper Hall.

By the early 1800s, however, the d'Arblay's ties with Surrey were broken and their further experiences in France and Brussels, though they make totally absorbing reading, are beyond the scope of this account. Fanny's beloved sister Susan, who had moved to Ireland with her increasingly unreliable husband, died in 1800 and, in 1810, while Fanny and Alexandre were still in France unable to return until 1812, William Lock died also. The sadness at that loss was compounded by the ungenerous action of William, his eldest son and his heir. He had continued to worry his father; accounted artistically very gifted, he was indolent and seemed completely without ambition. Writing to Gilpin in the 1780s, William Lock says how his son makes new resolutions 'yet, when the next day comes, it finds him as ill-disposed to labour as the preceding'.[13] Gilpin wrote to young William, trying to help, but to no avail and the latter's lack of interest in all that Norbury stood for was shown after his father's death when, having neglected the estate, he put it up for sale as too expensive to maintain. Next the astounded d'Arblays received a solicitor's letter stating that Camilla Cottage would also be sold. Despite earlier intentions, William Lock senior had never made out a legal transfer of the land and, although Alexandre and Fanny were offered compensation, it was a mere £700, which inevitably soured relations. Norbury Park has never had such a glittering span of years as when William Lock and Gilpin mused together over the picturesque, when Norbury was the centre of artists and art lovers, and a support for the émigrés and for the romance of the d'Arblays. 'Douce image de Norbury', wrote Madame de Staël in her heartfelt remembrance of the happiness she found there.

## NOTES TO CHAPTER VI

1   *Norbury Park Restoration Plan*, 1999, by Land Management Services Ltd. for Surrey County Council.
2   Rev. O. Manning and W. Bray, *The History and Antiquities of the County of Surrey* (London, 1804-14), vol. 4, p. 450 ff.
3   For this and further details of the Lock family, see the Duchess of Sermoneta, *The Locks of Norbury* (1940).
4   Correspondence, Bodleian Library, Eng. misc. d. 569; 572-5.
5   Ibid., 13 September 1781.
6   *Gentleman's Magazine*, October 1810, William Lock's obituary.
7   Charlotte Barrett (ed.), *Diary and Letters of Mme d'Arblay* (London, 1981), vol. 1, 23 April 1784.
8   Ibid., 25 October 1784.
9   Ibid., 9 November 1784.
10  Ibid., vol. 2, 24 July 1786. She continued in the Queen's service until 1791 when, very overstrained, she resigned.
11  Susan had been sent to Paris when she was nine, with an older sister, to board with a French family and learnt to speak French with ease.
12  These details and account of Fanny's sojourn in Surrey can be enjoyed from her letters and journals as edited by Joyce Hemlow and her assistants. See vols. 2 & 3 for Norbury and Great Bookham. *The Journals and Letters of Fanny Burney (Madame d'Arblay)* (Oxford, 1972-84).
13  Bodleian Library, as above, 19 March 1786.

# A NOTE ON CAMILLA LACEY

Camilla Cottage and its land was bought in 1816 by Thomas Hudson who greatly enlarged the house and added the local 'Lacey' to its name. Sold on again in 1874 to Leverton Wylie, it was in 1906 inherited by his nephew, Frederick Leverton Harris. An art lover and collector, he also much treasured his aunt and uncle's 'interesting collection of relics of Madame d'Arblay' housed 'in one of the old rooms' (*Surrey Archaeological Collections*, vol. x, 1890). But in 1919 a disastrous fire destroyed the building and of the collection there were only a few charred manuscript remains. Leverton Harris put the property up for sale and the house was rebuilt in 'Tudor' style. Considerably later, in 1931, after various vicissitudes, the estate was broken up into separate lots and sold off for development. Still called Camilla Lacey, the house now has no other connections with its origins.

CAMILLA LACEY. A BLACK AND WHITE WATERCOLOUR ON PENCIL, ARTIST UNKNOWN (1820S),
SHOWING THOMAS HUDSON'S ADDITIONS TO THE D'ARBLAYS' ORIGINAL SIMPLE MAISONETTE

NORBURY HOUSE, NORTH SIDE, *c.* 1916

THE CONSERVATORY AT NORBURY HOUSE, *c.* 1916
THIS WAS A FAVOURITE RESTING PLACE OF MARIE STOPES

# Chapter VII - Norbury after William Lock

THE Norbury estate was not sold until 1819 and, with quick changes of ownership, apart from improved access from the south side, it was not well maintained, as attested by John Timbs in 1823. He described the remains of a decayed greenhouse, trodden down parterres and several retired haunts 'in a wild and neglected state', though views were still 'of unparalleled richness'. However, in 1824, H. P. Sperling took over Norbury and stayed for over two decades, re-ordering the park, laying out the pleasure grounds afresh and opening up the prospect to the north-east by removing the upper crest of the chalk hill which had hitherto impeded the view. A less precipitous approach was engineered also on the north and, with the help of the local council, a bridge was constructed over the Mole to allow vehicular traffic, replacing the original footbridge.[1] Known as Weir Bridge, it is still in place and well-maintained.

WEIR BRIDGE AND LODGE *c.* 1916.
THE LODGE WAS DEMOLISHED IN 1937 TO MAKE WAY FOR THE NEW DUAL CARRIAGEWAY

Even more energetic was Sperling's successor, Thomas Grissell, a railway contractor by profession, who bequeathed in 1874 a much altered house and flourishing estate to his grandson. Refacing the building to give it a more classical appearance, adding pilasters, a parapet and cornices and extending the accommodation, 'the change was almost marvellous' said John Britton, the topographer. He was addressing a meeting at Norbury in 1849 and invited Thomas Grissell to plant a cedar tree on the lawn in front of the house to celebrate, quoting William Gilpin extensively whose praise of Norbury, he thought, was as applicable then as it had been in 1798.[2] Its beauty was further assured by Grissell's determination that the London Brighton and South Coast Railway should meet his require-ments if they were to construct their planned line between Horsham and Leatherhead which had to pass across a substantial part of his land. To keep the estate undisturbed, it was finally agreed that a tunnel should be bored through

WESTHUMBLE STATION

the chalk with no shafts for ventilation or other purpose admitted. Further, as Alan Jackson in his booklet *Dorking's Railways*[3] recounts, decorated structures had to be provided throughout - thus the three viaducts over the Mole had coloured brickwork, cornices and ornamented cast-iron parapets. A plantation of trees at least fifteen feet in height was to screen the north end of the tunnel and trees were to be put in and grass sown on all railway banks within sight of the house. Thomas Cubitt supported Grissell's demands and work started in 1864 with the line finally opening in 1867. The station at Westhumble, Thomas Grissell stipulated, had also to be of ornamental design and he reserved the right to halt the fast trains there at his convenience, to the pleasure of local residents if they happened to be returning home and saw his figure at Victoria Station. William Gilpin would certainly have considered the station with its curious steeply pitched roofs of patterned tiles and turret as 'ill-adapted', but it is well worth a visit in its now peaceful backwater.

After Thomas Grissell's death, the estate continued to be carefully maintained by his grandson, Thomas de la Garde Grissell[4] and equally prized by his successor, Leopold Salomons, who owned it from 1890 until 1914. There is an album of excellent photographs of Norbury at his time[5] showing the grounds and their unparalleled views, the gardens and the exterior and interior of the house. Of particular interest is the photograph of the painted drawing-room, showing the area to the right of the fireplace and the east wall's 'sylvan' scene, a noble work, as Gilpin described it, with its beautiful trees in the foreground, albeit somewhat obscured by the room's rather heavy furniture. The two wide-paned windows shown on the south side still call up the reality of the outside scene against the illusion within. The painted trellis round the ceiling is clearly depicted. Other photographs show the conservatory with its lavish planting, large palms and flowery banks, the gardens with trimmed yew hedges, ornamental bushes and flower borders lining the gravel walks, and the large rosery. This has a number of rose-beds surrounded by lawns and in its midst a statue of Diana and a playing fountain. The summer-house suggests a fitting resting place and the whole is encircled by luxuriant trees. There is an opulence about Victorian Norbury which was absent in William Lock's and Gilpin's time though the pleasure in its early days was as great.

Norbury, however, was about to enter its worst phase. Leopold Salomons, the benefactor of the National Trust (see chapter IV, note 17 on Box Hill) had planned also to bequeath Norbury to

THE MARBLE STATUE OF DIANA, THE HUNTRESS, WHEN IN THE CENTRE OF THE WATER-LILY POND IN THE 1930S

81

the nation but he died before he could complete the arrangements and in 1916 Sir Edward Mountain of Eagle Star acquired the property.

Over a decade of neglect followed when suddenly Norbury, 'one of the loveliest stretches of parkland in the Home Counties' as *The Times* of February 1930 wrote, was put up for auction and possible speculative housing development. This vandalism was rapidly averted by James Chuter Ede, at that time Chairman of Surrey County Council, who later became

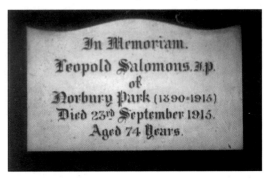

MEMORIAL PLAQUE TO LEOPOLD SALOMONS
IN MICKLEHAM CHURCH

well known nationally in his ministerial positions, first as Education Secretary (1940-5) and then as Home Secretary (1945-51). A great lover of the Mole Valley, he was appalled at Sir Edward Mountain's action. He heard the news only on the Friday afternoon with no possibility of consultation and took it upon himself to secure an option on the property, assuming personal responsibility for its purchase for £85,000. The risk was justified in that he received complete backing from the Council and it is entirely owing to him that Norbury was saved, apart from the house and its immediate land, as a prized part of the county's open space. Little did Thomas Grissell suspect how his determination to preserve his estate for himself, 'his heirs and assigns', would benefit the community.

JAMES CHUTER EDE BY MICHAEL NOAKES (1961)

The best known owners of Norbury House since 1930 are certainly H. V. Roe, who joined with his brother in aircraft manu-facturing (Avro) and his wife Marie Stopes, who has achieved lasting fame for her tireless work for women. Establishing birth-control clinics, lecturing and writing numerous books on motherhood and allied subjects, when they moved to Norbury in 1932, she worked from there with

MARIE STOPES ON THE STEPS FROM THE DINING-ROOM IN 1937

her two secretaries as often as she could, valuing the estate for itself, but also pleased with it for the status it gave. At the onset of World War II, with staff shortages and food rationing, she found herself increasingly involved in domestic affairs,[6] having, for instance, to hurry back from London to milk her two cows, Daffodil and Buttercup. She made her own butter, packets of which, on more than one occasion, she sent through the post to Walter de la Mare. She tended the geese and hens, complaining in

MARIE STOPES BY THE WATER-LILY POND

her letters of a mouse in their corn and of the hens' reluctance to lay, of Cowslip seizing her basket with its one collected egg and tossing it up in the air when she was not looking. She always loved her flowers - primrose time in the woods, the white broom 'like sunlit foam', the cascades of laburnum which made May and June espe-cially beautiful. She idolised her son but by then treated her loyal husband with scant respect. This, her second marriage, had been happy

83

enough in the past, but, a woman of ready feeling, she was apt to form strongly romantic attachments, this time to Keith Briant, much her junior, who, soon after the outbreak of the war, joined the Irish Guards. Very concerned about him until, eventually, she felt isolated by his marriage, she wrote him copious letters, speaking of the rose-garden and its Diana fountain where she could sit and recall his visits, the statue becoming an icon of her happiness. She banished it to the far end of the grounds later, in a fit of depression. Marie Stopes survived her husband by some years, dying of cancer in 1958, a rather saddened woman but unlikely in her pioneering work to be forgotten.

Although unhappily for us, the public, Norbury House has remained in private hands[7] so that the painted drawing-room is rarely seen, much good work has taken place in the rest of the park. Under a ten-year plan and now with a new management initiative, *2000-2005*, the area is well served. An excellent illustrated booklet, the *Management Trail*, is available which is valuable for the specialist and the Surrey country-lover alike. It describes a way-marked circular walk giving a clear picture of planting, growth and planned felling of trees at Norbury and the wildlife to be found there. Past history, too, is being preserved in that the original view lines down the combs of the hills, which Gilpin found so satisfyingly picturesque, have been identified and it is intended to re-open the footpaths along the contours of the hillside. Once again, it will be possible to see views through the spreading arms of the trees 'acting as the frame of a picture', as he noted in 1775.

NOTES TO CHAPTER VII

1   For details of these years see E. W. Brayley and J. Britton, *Topographical history of Surrey* (London, 1825-6), vol. 4, pp. 448, 452-4.
2   J. Britton's *Autobiography* (1849-50), vol. 2, p. 110 ff. 1798 refers to the publication date of Gilpin's *Western Tour*.
3   Alan A Jackson, *Dorking's Railways* (Dorking Local History Group, 1988).
4   *Gardeners Chronicle*, vol. i, (1882), p. 667 ff.
5   Album held at Surrey History Centre. For drawing room and conservatory see *supra* pp. 69 and 78.
6   For Marie Stopes' life at Norbury Park see her letters, British Library, especially Add.: MSS. 58501 and 58537. A very readable biography is Ruth Hall, *Marie Stopes* (Deutsch, 1977).
7   Marie Stopes bequeathed Norbury to the Royal Society of Literature, but they sold it on to private buyers. (Information kindly supplied by Dr. Stopes-Roe).

A chatty but useful background account of the area, including further details of Camilla Lacey, is contained in *Mickleham the Story of a Parish* by Ronald Shepperd (Mickleham Publications, 1991).

# CHAPTER VIII
## RETURN TO CHEAM, PASSING 'MR HOWARD'S PARK'

*'From Leatherhead the road leads through common fields to Asted: From thence through a lane, with Mr Howard's park wall on the right. On leaving Asted, it rises up an hill, through a common, in which nothing is striking.*

*'At the top of the hill is a fine view of Epsom, and the Downs beyond it.*

*'On leaving Epsom, the road gets again in common fields.'*

EXTRACT FROM JOHN ROCQUE,
*MAP OF SURREY* (1768)

## ASHTEAD PARK

MR (Sir Robert) Howard's park wall, dating from the 1680s is still unmissable, encompassing as it does all the area to Rookery Hill. This road marks the boundary which divides the grounds of the City of London Freemen's School from the remaining section of Ashtead Park. Fringed now by Surrey suburbia, the result of building plots sold off in the 1920s, this is managed by the Mole Valley District Council as a nature reserve and public park. Both areas are much the same in size measuring about 57 acres (23 hectares).

Ashtead Park has had a most interesting history from the time when Sir Robert Howard bought the manor in 1680 with its small deer park from his cousin Henry Howard, the sixth Duke of Norfolk,[1] and turned the whole into a gentleman's estate. Ashtead was sufficiently accessible to London to suit his literary, artistic and political activities - he was an MP and Auditor of the Exchequer for the major part of his career.[2] Sir Robert built a new house which William Gilpin in his *Western Tour* described as 'not grand but

*A SCENE IN ASHTED PARK* BY THOMAS HEARNE (1744-1817).
ETCHING. ENGRAVED BY LETITIA BYRNE (1805)

compact and comfortable',[3] which replaced the old manor house adjoining the church. Its layout and gardens were formal and typical of the time; a lime walk connected the house with the church and, in the park, Sir Robert 'planted largely' - a hundred years later Gilpin was to note the fine oaks and elms that ornamented the varied and undulating grounds.[5] A lime avenue stretched from the front carriage area through the entrance gates and continued to join the London road further on. This 'exceedingly pleased' John Evelyn as he rode along it in 1684 to visit Sir Robert at 'his very sweet park upon the down'.[6] It was Sir Robert, too, who excavated the small lake known as Island Pond, now cleared again, just beyond Rookery Hill. Sir Robert died in 1698 and his son inherited, Ashtead Park remaining in Howard hands for nearly another two centuries.

'The house is now rebuilt', adds William Gilpin in a note to the published edition of his same *Western Tour*. The rebuilding was carried out in the early 1790s[7] by Richard Bagot who had married Frances Howard and taken her name. On the old site a handsome Italianate mansion was constructed, designed by Bonomi, which has happily survived, as has, if much altered, a grand stable-block to the west. To the 'majestically timbered deer-park' he added more land; the later gardens took shape, the east side under his daughter Mary's care becoming a formal rose and scented flower garden.[8] Shrubberies, new young trees including cedars, were added and, during the nineteenth century, the kitchen gardens and the glasshouses reached near perfection.

When the house was sold in 1879 to Sir Thomas Lucas,[9] he also prized the estate. A rich engineer and art lover, he did not spare expense. New balustrading round the house and the impressive iron gates at the entrance to what is now the public park were among his improvements. Either he or his successor Pantia Ralli, of the Greek shipping family, the documentation is unclear, added wings to the mansion, the east wing holding a marble floored conservatory with a marble goldfish basin and an indoor rockery. Ralli was certainly lavish in his expenditure.[10] From 1889-1924 he oversaw the making of further walks and gardens - he established the attractive topiary garden on the north front which is still a showpiece today, he arranged mass plantings, including bulbs and exotic shrubs, and the construction of a second lake, the 'Boathouse' pond. Mr Ralli's hospitality locally was renowned and, of his herd of one hundred and fifty deer, he culled fifteen annually to distribute to his friends.

On his death in 1924 all this came to an abrupt end. The whole estate was put up for sale, in fifty-one separate lots, for housing development. Fortunately, as already noted, the Corporation of London purchased the mansion and considerable adjoining land for their new school building

THE MANSION, ASHTEAD PARK, FROM THE 1880 SALE PARTICULARS

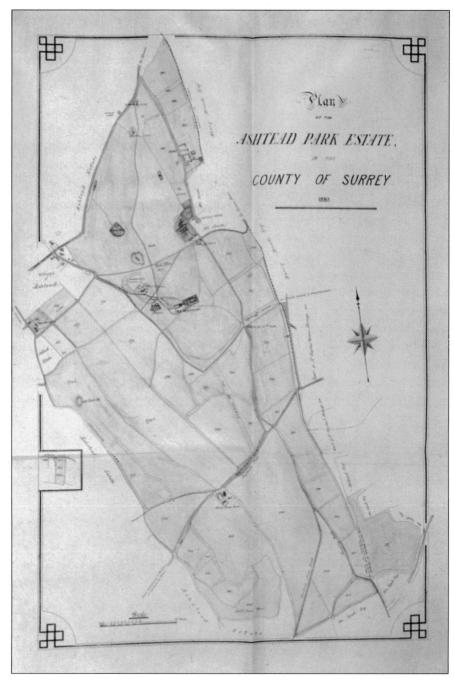

ASHTEAD PARK ESTATE IN 1880

and, twenty years later, through direct recommendation of the Abercrombie Report,[11] further sale of building sites was stopped and other development already agreed upon cancelled. In the school grounds there are still

THE TOPIARY GARDEN

indications of early woodland paths, though open ground has been levelled for playing-fields. The lovely south avenue is still there with young limes well established after the destruction by the 1987 hurricane. Beyond Rookery Hill a path leads to the Island Pond where wild birds, especially herons, can be observed and one can sense something of the original ample park from the forest trees and relics of earlier planting. It is a peaceful atmosphere such as William Gilpin would have enjoyed.

ASHTEAD PARK HOUSE IN 2000

R IDING across a further common Gilpin arrives at the top of the hill from which he admires the view of Epsom and the downs beyond it. Of Epsom itself he had no great opinion. John Toland, who wrote about it earlier in the century in the highest terms, he dismisses[12] as exercising 'the powers of a wanton imagination with more innocence on this subject than on many others. All that can now be said of it [Epsom] with truth . . . is that it is a large pleasant village,' its chief recommendation being its situation on the skirts of Banstead Downs. They, apart from their sports and their mutton, were adorned, he thought, with 'rich and very picturesque distances'.

On that note, which reminds us of the enjoyment William Gilpin had on his holidays in selecting and recording the Picturesque in our countryside - a keen pleasure he hoped 'not inconsistent with the profession of a clergyman' - we leave him as he rides back to Cheam and his school.

## NOTES TO CHAPTER VIII

1   Symmes' *Collections for Surrey*, British Library, Add: MS 6167, f. 49.
2   H. J. Oliver, *Sir Robert Howard* (Duke University Press, 1963) gives interesting details of Sir Robert at Ashtead.
3   *Western Tour*, pp. 5-6.
4   For further information of the estate see Revd. F.E. Paget, *Some Records of the Ashtead Estate and of its Howard Possessors* (1873, privately printed).
5   *Western Tour*, p. 3. Gilpin also speaks of the property as being 'within a walled circumference of about two miles'.
6   E. S. de Beer (ed.), John Evelyn's *Diary*, vol. 4, 10 May 1684.
7   Paget, p. 169 ff.
8   John Loudon, *The Gardener's Magazine* (October 1829).
9   Sir Thomas Lucas (1822-1902) was created Baronet in 1887. His firm was connected with the construction of Cannon Street Station and Alexandra Palace, among other work.
10  A good description of the gardens in Pantia Ralli's time is in the *Journal of Horticulture and Cottage Gardener* (February 1900) and in the *Gardeners' Chronicle* (October 1914).
11  The Abercrombie Committee set out its post-war plan for Greater London in 1944. Of Ashtead Park it says 'As much [land] as possible should be kept open to form a break between Ashtead and Epsom. The development . . . should be abandoned and permission to develop cancelled'. (Section 409).
12  *Western Tour*, p. 6.

# APPENDIX - THE TEXT

## RYGATE - DORKING
### The Rookery
### Aug 24, 1768

## TO RYGATE, FROM THENCE TO DORKING, AND TO CHEAM

'Over the Downs to Potter's Lane is about three miles. The Downs afford no great variety. The ground in many parts is beautifully laid out; the furzy part contrasts with the smooth; the eye is in many places agreeably entertained with winding roads, traversing the heath in various directions; and the edge of the whole is pleasantly skirted with wood; among which the spire of Bansted is an object. At the entrance of Potter's Lane, if you turn round, you have a view nobly extensive. The distant parts of it melt entirely into an ocean of air. From that downy height you are considerably raised above the country, and have a stretch of many leagues before you. The parts are pleasantly blended; but not enough separated. You do not see that pleasing difference between wood and plain, which is so agreeable in a landskip; and which catches large bodies of light: *Late discriminat agros.*[*] There is a want too of objects. St Paul's is a very fine one; but there is nothing else of use in the way, except Wimbledon-house; and that only when the sun shines upon it. Indeed St Paul's and Wimbledon are both too insignificant. In such an expanse as this there should be several objects; and at different distances, some within three, four or five miles of the eye which would give them strength, and consequence in the landskip. These are removed 14 or 15 miles. In short, the beauty of the view consists principally in its vastness, and in the agreeable contrast it makes with the smooth surface of the Downs.

'As you go up Potter's Lane, you have catches of the same country, on the left; which being seen through the hedge-row trees, and having the advantage of foreground, appear to more advantage.

'On the entrance of Walton-heath you have a wild and desolate view. Nothing can be more dreary, and comfortless. Nor is there the least catch of distant country to shew you that you are in a cultivated land. A solitary wind-

---

*Virgil, *Aeneid*, Book XI, 144, describing how the flames from the Arcadians lighted the road and 'far and wide threw up the outlines of the field'.

mill, and a spire, on the right, just tell you that the country is inhabited. In a mile's riding you come to a dip in the heath, which lets in a little of the country, and adds some variety.

'At the turnpike, which is about 4 miles from Ryegate, you get into an open lane, which is not unpleasant. The views towards Gatton, on the left, serve you to range over, till that vast expanse of country breaks in upon you, from the top of Ryegate-hill. The parts are in general larger, than the view from Potter's Lane; and in some places the distance is very picturesque.

'From Ryegate towards Dorking you pass over a common about half a mile; at the close of which you have a picturesque view. A good foreground of trees, and broken ground, with a winding road, a first distance of woody hedgerows well grouped and shapen; beyond them a second distance of rising ground. From hence you enter into a close lane; some part of it very close, rocky on each side, over-hung thick with wood, dark and gloomy. In many parts you have agreeable catches of hilly ground, which in some places appear to great advantage over trees. On the left Beachworth-castle, rising among wood, makes a beautiful object, and puts you in mind of Poussin. Another view of it presents itself, through an opening of the hedge, still more picturesque than the last; only it is in some degree hurt by the regularity of a row of trees, which should be cut up, or broken, to make the view quite agreeable.

'Over the bridge over the Mole, the view is pleasant. The river forms a little contracted bay, shadowed round with wood. Beyond appears at a distance on an eminence Mr King's house, (formerly Tyre's) which at that distance has the appearance of a castle. The landscape is such as would suit Berghem's pencil. Fill the water with cattle coolling [sic] their toes; place a shepherd on the shore with a female peasant, a dog, and 2 or 3 cows; give the sky a glow, and you have one of his pictures.

'At Dorking I swallowed a dish of tea, and got into a chaise for the Rookery, leaving my horse to bait. (NB Here the Rookery).

## THE ROOKERY NEAR DORKING IN SURREY

'The late proprietor of the place, Mr Malthouse, found, I was told, a mere wilderness. The ground-plot is a valley between two woody hills. Part of the valley was watery. The hills were a thicket; and the water a bed of sedge. He has literally done nothing but remove <u>deformities</u>, and add <u>variety</u>. The water he has cleared, and formed into a lake: the woods he has opened in many places; and exhibited a variety of lawns, open groves, and close recesses. Everything is grand, simple, and uniform; the purest nature I ever met with in any improvement. At Stow, at Kew, at Painshill, you see the greatest profusion of expence. You every where see the hand of art: Nature never makes her excursions in such polished walks; plants her shrubberies, and her ever-greens in such artificial combinations; and brings vistas, and objects together with so much forced antithesis. But in all the beautiful sylvan scenes here exhibited nothing is introduced, but what nature herself might be supposed to create.Where you have a barren spot to improve, you must do the best you can: but certainly the simple scenes of pure nature have something ravishing in them, which art can never produce.

'It would require long examination to criticise particularly each of the beautiful scenes here exhibited. Those which struck me most were the following.

'The lake is one. It covers, I should imagine, about half a dozen acres. The water, surrounded on every side by hanging woods, rising from the very edge, doubles a promontary of beach, and alders, opens in a second bay upon an island, on which stands a temple dedicated to Venus. The whole scene is a noble amphitheatre, and infinitely pleasing. Such a piece of simple nature far excells any made water, tho the margin be formed by a line ever so various; and the extremities ever so artificially concealed. This scene is as grand as any thing within such narrow limits can be. The largeness of the parts gives an idea of vastness much beyond its size. If any thing in it is displeasing, it is the temple, which is in itself no beautiful object, and is besides ill-adapted. If there must be an object, a naid-grotto, quite simple, had been more suitable.

'The ground about the temple of Pan is another very beautiful scene. It is a sloping lawn, skirted with wood. At the upper end stands the temple, well adapted to the situation; which is just such a retreat as a shepherd might be supposed to choose for his flock at noon, or evening, affording both pasturage, and shelter. The building (formed of stumps, and moss, and thatched with chips) is wholly artless, and simple. It is indeed an imitation of Grecian architecture: but Pan himself, it might be supposed, or some of his rustic worshippers might have seen the form, and imitated it with such materials as they found upon the spot. Had it been constructed of hewn stone it had lost its simplicity.

'The temple of Sylvanus affords another very beautiful scene, still more picturesque than the last. It stands nearly upon the knowl of a woody hill; shaded by trees, and open only in two directions. In front the hill slopes gradually along a lawn, into an open grove; through which it sinks into a dark wood. In the other direction the hill falls precipitately; and through the boles of lofty trees you have a beautiful view of a rich country. Such a foreground gives it the spirit of a landscape. The situation is well adapted to the inhabitant.

The place naturally suggests the idea of a wild wood-god, just peeping out to take a distant view of the world, darting instantly into his thicket, if any thing alarm him. This habitation is properly furnished with bows and arrows, oaten-pipes, and instruments of husbandry.

'The Hermitage affords another very beautiful scene, and wholly different from any of the others. It stands upon the steep side of one woody hill, and overlooks another so that the prospect is entirely woody. You look down a precipice, and see nothing but the boles of trees, and brushwood at the bottom: you look across the valley, and take in a short distance; but it is a distance composed only of the foliage of trees seen through the branches of those more at hand. The whole scene is grand, and solemn; the world, and every concern in it, is shut out; and nothing left the hermit, but the heavens to contemplate.

'From the gloomy scene, you enter into open day, where the last grand prospect breaks in upon you. You see on one side, the smooth declivity of an hill skirted with wood; on the other, a noble tent of hanging woods rising above the trees of the valley.

'To take a thorough view of all the beauties of the very rich spot, carries you a round of about 5 miles. There are, besides these, very many very beautiful scenes; but these were the most striking.

'A spot in the wood, dedicated to the genius of Socrates, seems to me no way adapted.

'Near Dorking, at Dibden, Mr Howard, heir to the D. of Norfolk, is building a very handsome house. It stands high; is skreened by a wood behind it, and commands a noble view of the vale of the Mole, of which the boundary is Boxhill, which seen in perspective is a fine object. The other parts of the view are not very picturesque.

'From Dorking to Mickleham, and from thence to Leatherhead, is the sweetest ride imaginable. Box-hill is a grand object on the right, which accompanies you great part of the way. In itself it is [a] large, mishapen mass - vast, unbroken denseness(?) with little variety. The first part of it is covered with box; it then shows the chalk in large shelving currents from its sides(?), the box struggling with the chalk: the third part of it is a downy declivity. The line at the top in every part almost unbroken; and has as little variety as so long a line almost can have. The Mole runs at the bottom of it, but is hid from the eye by the hedges of the lane. The large trees which grow upon the banks of the river are of great service in giving space and distance to the hill. It is seen best just at the end of Dorking where it appears in proper perspective. On the left Lady Trion's park affords a beautiful view. It is a rising lawn of

94

firm turf ornamented with clumps. On the right, we passed by a low thatched cottage, lately belonging to Mr Re . . . , on which a great deal of money has been thrown away. It is full of littlenesses and trifling objects. It might be made a pretty place if every thing was undone which has been done.

'From Mickleham the high grounds on the right, and the meadows on the left, through which the Mole flows, whose course is marked by lofty alders make a pleasing contrast.

'From Leatherhead the road leads through common fields to Asted: From thence through a lane, with Mr Howard's park wall on the right. On leaving Asted, it rises up an hill, through a common, in which nothing is striking.

'At the top of the hill is a fine view of Epsom, and the Downs beyond it.

'On leaving Epsom, the road gets again in common fields.'

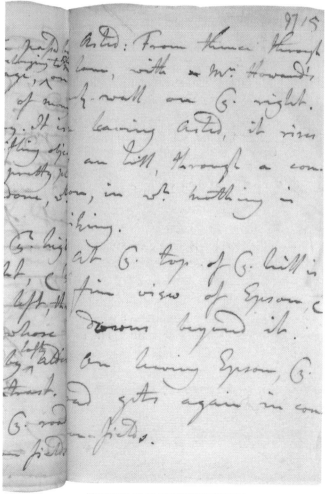

THE FINAL PAGE OF THE MANUSCRIPT

95

# Bibliographical Information

Below is the list of William Gilpin's works used in this account. All other sources are listed in the bibliographical notes following the chapters or are referred to directly in the chapters themselves.

*A Dialogue upon the Gardens of the Right Honourable The Lord Viscount Cobham, at Stow in Buckinghamshire*, London, 1748, published anonymously. (Abbrev: *Stowe Dialogue*)

*An Essay on Prints*, 1781. This is the third edition and the first to bear Gilpin's name. (1st edition 1768)

*Observations on the River Wye and several parts of South Wales, etc. relative chiefly to Picturesque Beauty; made in the summer of the year 1770*, London, 1782. (Abbrev: *Wye Tour*)

*Observations, on Several Parts of England, particularly the Mountains and Lakes of Cumberland and Westmoreland, relative chiefly to Picturesque Beauty, made in the year 1772*. Two vols., London, 1786. (Abbrev: *Lakes Tour*)

*Observations on the Western Parts of England, relative chiefly to Picturesque Beauty. To which are added, a Few Remarks on the Picturesque Beauties of the Isle of Wight*, London, 1798. (Abbrev: *Western Tour*)

*Remarks on Forest Scenery, and other Woodland Views, relative chiefly to Picturesque Beauty illustrated by the Scenes of New Forest in Hampshire*. Two vols., London, 1791. (Abbrev: *Forest Scenery*)

*Three Essays: On Picturesque Beauty; On Picturesque Travel; and on Sketching Landscape; To which is added a poem, On Landscape Painting*, London, 1792. (Abbrev: *Three Essays*)

# LIST OF MAPS AND ILLUSTRATIONS

NOTE: Items marked SHC are the copyright of the Surrey History Centre and are reproduced with their kind permission. We are especially grateful to be allowed to reproduce, in some cases for the first time, illustrative material taken from six portfolios of views of Surrey compiled by Robert Barclay of Bury Hill, Dorking, early in the nineteenth century. This was intended to extra-illustrate his copy of Revd. O. Manning and W. Bray, *The History and Antiquities of the County of Surrey*, published in three volumes between 1804-1814, and was purchased by the then Surrey Record Office in March 1995. These are items referenced SHC 4348. We are also grateful to the other sources listed for permission to use their material.

# INDEX

NOTES: In references Revd. William Gilpin has been abbreviated to WG. References to illustrations and their captions are indicated by **bold type**